The Son with Two Moms

By

Anthony M. Hynes

Acknowledgments

To my professor and friend, Kimberly Moffitt, without you my journey is not one I would have begun, much less finished. You helped me realize my story was worth telling. To my editor Andrea Grenadier, for helping me reach the finish line with your wonderful edits and your beautiful encouragement. You are truly one of a kind. To Troy Wiipongwii, my friend and brother, for being honest about every aspect of the manuscript, and for making sure I was giving the truest representation of myself to my readers. To my sister, Angela Jones, the most genuine person I know. Your smile still lights up a room and your spirit lifts me up. You remind me who I am and who I strive to be like. To Colleen Jones, my mother and protector; you are the truest example of human kindness. I am your son and every time someone comments about how nice I am, I think of you. Your aura fills a room and changes it into a better place. To Janet Marjorie Simons and Mary Gwen Hynes, my moms; your love, courage, strength, resilience, intelligence, and tireless work ethic are things I still admire. You will forever be in my heart, and forever a part of how I live my life.

Preface

As of 2012, there were 110,000 children living in same-sex households. This book is a testament to those children. Every one of us has a different story. I can't wait to hear theirs.

Chapter 1: Reality

I was recently asked, "What is the biggest obstacle you have ever had to overcome?" I answered the question by stating that losing my mother was the most difficult thing I have ever had to endure. I love her, and losing her had always been my worst nightmare. She is the person who is most like me; it's as if we were modeled after one another. I was very close to her and she was very close to me – she told me so in her days of living, and left her journal behind as a reminder. It was a journal she never mentioned keeping, and one that I didn't stumble upon for over 13 years after this first paragraph was written. It reads:

> *"I'm 33 years old. I have a good marriage, a beautiful 7 and a half year old son, a rewarding career and many friends; I'm financially comfortable but not wealthy. My needs aren't extravagant. I've always enjoyed good health, even excellent health. I also have cancer."*

The entry is dated May 7, 1997. A few days later, my mom asked me if I had ever heard of something called "cancer." And from that point, I faced the toughest trial life has ever given me.

Chapter 2: Writing on the Wall

I found Mary's journal while cleaning the living room during one of those hot, muggy August days. I rifled through mounds of musty envelopes containing bank statements, came across a *Time* magazine article detailing how the U.S. was going to respond to 9/11, and found a couple of old books detailing the race problem in America. It had been a long day of cleaning, and yet I was enjoying having something to do. I didn't have a job, my college credit summer class had ended weeks ago, and it was two in the afternoon; much too early for my daily rendezvous with neighborhood friends. After watching several episodes of the show *Supernatural,* I decided that it was time to do some work. I had made cleaning the entire house by the end of the summer my goal and I intended to reach that goal.

The whole place had been a cluttered mess ever since Mary began her prolonged hospital stays. She was our rock when it came to housekeeping. She vacuumed, cooked, and scrubbed her way into our hearts. With her gone, Janet and I were left to fend for ourselves, which we did poorly. Our food dynamic in particular changed abruptly, and takeout took precedence over the homemade pasta and chicken pot pie that Mary had been so fond of making. In her absence, Janet and I became resourceful takeout carnivores. Rotisserie chicken was often our dinner of choice.

On a typical night we would eat in the den. Behind us sits a framed caricature of two women and a little boy at the beach.

Black wooden TV trays sit in front of us as our eyes stay glued to the tube. NBC is the channel and *Law & Order* is the show. Janet sets down a book on the now-empty TV tray. The book sits atop one of my old *Sports Illustrated* magazines, which covers an old *Newsweek.*

Neither of us has enough energy to move. By the end of the month, the TV tray is stacked to capacity, and we have another TV tray simply for food.

In a few weeks, the chairs in the living room had books on them, the couch had books on it, the table where mama used to serve dinner had books on it, and Mary's side of the bed was covered with books. For 10 years our house was clean and organized, now our home had become complete chaos. However, I am grateful for the chaos, which allowed me to find a lost treasure, a piece of writing that I was meant to find as a young adult rather than as a small child. That very first paragraph summed up how Mary was feeling at the time – a time when she did not feel comfortable expressing her true emotions to her young son.

> *I'm 33 years old. I have a good marriage, a beautiful 7 and a half year old son, a rewarding career and many friends; I'm financially comfortable but not wealthy. My needs aren't extravagant. I've always enjoyed good health, even excellent health. I also have cancer."*

The words still echo in my mind, bringing a chill over me as they did on that hot August day, so many seasons ago.

Chapter 3: The Family

If I am close to someone, I want them to know every aspect that has shaped me as a man, which is why I only tell a select group of people about myself. You are now one of those people. By telling my story I am giving you a part of myself.

Our family came to be on March 26, 1992, when a couple took me out of St. Ann's, an orphanage in Washington, D.C. They had been together for several years and wanted to start a family. One was a lawyer who worked at a firm in Washington, D.C., and the other a data analyst for the Children's Defense Fund, an organization devoted to protecting the rights of children. The two had been going out for a couple of years, and were deeply in love. They were not married yet, but had exchanged informal vows.

The adoption was my mother, Mary's, idea; my other mother, Janet, was career driven and was unsure if bringing a child into the picture was the right move. However, Mary's love proved convincing enough, and by the end of January, they had decided to raise a child together.

Both Mary and Janet had had difficult and somewhat distant relationships with their own parents, but together they knew that they were strong enough to raise a child. They decided upon adoption, and took the necessary steps to ensure it would happen. They procured a lawyer to oversee the process, and went to work finding a suitable child. They would soon discover that a child would be assigned to them based on availability alone, and would have to take whomever was selected for them.

Several long weeks rolled by before they finally received the call they were waiting for. A child by the name of Tony Lee Jones was now available for adoption, and was only 2 ½years old. They were shown a picture of the little guy and decided to visit him.

A few days later, they were driving their small, red car up the road, ready for their adventure. They stepped out of the car slowly, walking up the brown steps, before slowly pushing open an old wooden door. Upon entering, they were greeted by the sight of several dozen cribs adorned with the things babies and toddlers enjoy. There were Legos. There were cotton blankets with ducks on them and there were colorful rattles strewn all over the place, items which they took great care to avoid as they made their way to Tony's crib.

Both prospective parents were anxious. After all, they had received only background information on the little fellow, and had no idea what type of situation they were walking into. For instance, they knew that he was just over 2 years old, had been living in St. Ann's for 1 year, and that he was given up for adoption by a single mother named Colleen Jones who suffered from schizophrenia. They knew that he had a sister, Angela, who was 9 years older than him, and who lived with his step great aunt. They knew Angela was not interested in being adopted, but still wanted to see Tony whenever it was possible. However, they knew nothing of Tony's medical history, who his father was, or what his favorite food happened to be (chicken nuggets).

However, the sullen, brown face staring at them from the small blue crib was an arresting one. His almond-shaped, brown eyes had a kind but piercing nature about them, and his puffy cheeks stood out as the grownups tried to bargain a grin out of him. The corners of his mouth never twitched into a smile, even with continued baby talk and cooing. Still, despite this minor setback, the couple decided to see him again.

Several days later, they took Tony to the playground to see how he interacted with them. It took a little time, but eventually he started warming up to each of them. He started to smile, even laughing at times. He never spoke, but the warmth they felt around him said volumes about their budding relationship.

Before long, they were taking him to other places: the zoo, the park where he could zip around on the swings, laughing wildly as Mary and Janet anxiously smiled. He went to the movies with them, his eyes transfixed on the man riding on a flying carpet. He came to the house and stayed the night with them, eating cupcakes and listening to Motown. Indeed, in a sense, this child was rented to the couple for 2 days on a short-term lease. They liked him so much, they decided to see him again a week or two later. By the third and fourth visits, they realized that they had to have him, and on March 26, 1992, Mary and Janet took him home to stay.

Chapter 4: Early Beginnings

I cannot recall the first few months living with my parents. However, Janet helped me fill in the pieces. For example, I was apparently horribly afraid of cats at the time. Whenever Amstel and Sixpack (Mary's idea for names) walked up to me I ran away quickly, afraid of what those big claws would do to me. I had never seen a cat before, and after my first few encounters with one I never wanted to see one again. Somehow though, I managed to live—and what a great life it became.

I went to the playground, played with clay, and kicked the soccer ball around until it was too dark to see it. By the time Janet and Mary tucked me in to bed, my eyes were half closed, exhausted from the afternoon's exploits. I woke up the next morning with the energy that only a 3 -year-old could possess, ready to take on the day. Janet and Mary would call me downstairs for breakfast, where an old plate topped with bacon and scrambled eggs awaited me. Janet stood by the counter, hunched over as she prepared my peanut butter and jelly sandwich. Mary reached above the refrigerator for her coffee, moving much slower than her years would suggest. Both women looked at me wearily, contemplating how they were going to make it through another day with such a rambunctious child.

Luckily for them, their services were often not needed. Several other kids my age roamed the neighborhood, and I chose to expend my energy with them, racing out of the door as Mary and Janet lingered behind.

There were a half-dozen boys my age in the neighborhood, but the children I saw most were Devin and Pat, whose small brick house was located at the top of the block. Pat was 6 months my senior, Devin 9 months my junior.

The two looked more like friends than brothers. Devin had freckles, Pat did not. Devin was skinny, Pat was not. Pat was really into technology, Devin was not. Pat was cerebral, short tempered, and passionate. Devin was laid back, even keeled, and unflappable. The love they had for each other, however, was mutual, and it was this that made them brothers.

The three of us became best friends, and trolled 16th Avenue without a care, playing street hockey, Wiffle Ball, basketball, and soccer whenever we had the opportunity. By the time dinner rolled around, we had worked up quite an appetite, and sat down to eat with vigor.

The location of our evening feast rotated between our two houses. Tuesday night I might have gone to Devin and Pat's house for chicken and Thursday they might have come to my house for burgers. There was no set schedule, but it was understood that each household would cook for an additional hungry boy or two on any given night.

Both families welcomed each other with open arms, and our parents became friends as well, the 30-something Irish Catholic couple and the two lesbians separated by 20 years. Perhaps it was this that they joked about as their loud laughter echoed through the floor boards and into the den where Devin, Pat, and I sat.

However, they could have been as loud as a cannon before we realized noise of any kind was being made. We were occupied with our beloved Mortal Combat and NBA Jamz PlayStation games. Our world was one in which grownups were not allowed in on Friday nights without a pizza in hand, preferably from Tony's Villa.

After we ate, we mindlessly returned our gaze to the TV screen without acknowledging our parents' presence. We had a system in place in which whoever wasn't playing took the time to eat their pizza while the other two played. In actuality, this was less of a system and more of what just happened every time we were given food in the middle of games. Once in a while we paused the game to turn to the Friday night lineup on ABC. I remember the shows included *Boy Meets World* and *Family Matters,* two of our favorites.

Shortly after the programs ended, I parted ways with Devin and Pat, only to return the next day to pick up where we left off.

***

Despite how close we were, Devin, Pat and I did not attend the same school. Pat went to a different kindergarten than Devin attended, and for grade school, Devin and Pat went to a different school than I did. Still, we always managed to make up for lost time when we were together. They made my transition into my new surroundings that much easier, and together we fostered each others' interests in sports. All of us loved running, jumping, and kicking, and after a period, learned how to do all three at the same time.

Their father, Dennis, was a big part of our athletic development as well. I swear a quarter of the first 10 years of my life consisted of riding in Dennis' white Toyota pickup truck on the way to the gym or field to play in some sporting event. In basketball he taught us how to shoot, and in soccer he coached our very first team with Mary, one of my two moms, who proved to be no slouch athletically.

Dennis had never played organized soccer a day in his life. However, that didn't stop him from being the best soccer coach possible. He set up shop, kneeling on the sideline with a Dunkin Donuts coffee in hand. I honestly have no idea what drills we ran or how we were told to kick the ball. For all I know, all of Dennis's remarks came down to "kick" and "run." However, to a 5-year-old, these were vital pieces of information. All of us kicked and ran as hard as our little feet could tolerate.

For me, though, the experience out on the field amounted to more than just running and kicking. When I was out there, I became more assertive and confident. Soccer became the ultimate adrenaline rush, a place where the only thing that mattered was releasing fury. Most people equate releasing anger with hitting something, but for me it was more than that.

Being on the pitch allowed me to hone my anger, to will it into energy. That anger was due to how different I felt my life was. My family was not normal, which was fine. What was not fine was the chip on my shoulder I felt every day. I was angry I did not have a father. I was angry at being overlooked, at being put in an orphanage. That energy helped me beat a defender to the ball, shrug a would-be tackler off the ball, and bark orders to the midfielders not getting back on defense fast enough. That energy made me a leader, and that energy forced me to step out of my shell to the point where I forgot I'd had one. That energy turned me into a leader, a boy who could block everything out and focus on everything in between the two goal posts set before him. A well-timed tackle, a perfect shielding of the ball, a furious run around and through two defenders, made me feel like a warrior, and a warrior is always in control. However, this energy allowed me to do something else too—have fun. Making people miss, gliding up the sideline for a pass, putting the ball in the goal and seeing it go *whoosh* in that white net? *Priceless*.

Chapter 5: Soccer

Soccer. Futbol! Was and is my favorite sport to this very day. I am told that I was given a small size-one soccer ball at the age of three, and the rest is history.

Mary and Janet had no prior knowledge of anything soccer related before I joined the family. Janet is a former resident of New York City and so she knew that Pelé came to play for the New York Cosmos in the 1970s; however, that was pretty much it when it came to her knowledge of the sport. For her part, Mary knew as much about soccer as Pelé's dog. So clearly, they knew they were in over their heads in the soccer arena, but persisted anyway. Both took up dedicated posts devoted to making sure I was prepped and ready for my soccer-related adventures. Janet was responsible for getting all of my soccer gear. She helped me pick out shin guards and the like. Mary, on the other hand, was the one who directed my 4-year-old "training" sessions. We took turns kicking the ball back and forth to one another while she shouted words of encouragement. One portion of the front lawn always ended up a paler shade of green than the rest of the yard, a battle scar from our soccer exploits.

One of my first soccer teams was a club simply known as "The Gold Team." Before our first game I reached into our big cardboard box and plucked a jersey emblazoned with a "4" on the back, a tradition for years to come.

Our team played in the Takoma Park Rec League, a team filled with kids from Takoma Park and the surrounding area. We played every Saturday morning, our fall seasons lasting until the first freeze in early December, and our spring seasons lasting until the first 90-degree days in June.

For the parents, soccer represented a time for rest and relaxation as they watched their children gallop around the pitch. However, now that I am older, I realize that Saturday mornings must have been a living hell for many of them. After a long week at work, I am certain the last thing they wished to be doing was to wake up early on a Saturday morning to attend their children's soccer games. However, it was their duty, and so they went to battle every Saturday morning, asserting their will on an enemy infused with high sugar levels and creative coloring books.

In our household, Mary or Janet spent half the morning tracking down my soccer socks, finding my shin guards, and making a big breakfast so I would have the energy to run around for 40 minutes without collapsing. I was disorganized, so it was unlikely that I was ready to leave when my parents wanted to leave. I also had a youthful arrogance, and so it was unlikely that I cared how many minutes before game time I showed up, as long as I arrived.

For my moms, as well as all of the other parents in attendance, watching the actual game on Saturday must have been like sitting back and enjoying a great meal they spent hours preparing. The games must have felt like relaxed social gatherings. The backdrop of soccer matches were a chance to swap horror stories of raising children, share a few coffees, and enjoy each others' company.

For the kids, every touch of the ball was supposed to be seen by the select parent in attendance and praised accordingly. I for one surely believed Janet and Mary were watching my every play, when in all likelihood they were tuning in and out whenever the moment called for it. "Yea!" Great play, honey!" They would enthusiastically say.

Still, it was always nice to have them there, and they each seemed to get a kick out of watching me play. It was fun, and all of my teammates were nice. I always looked forward to going out for pizza with them after our post-game oranges were served. Each Saturday was magnificent because, win or lose, we went.

Some may say that our parents set a bad precedent for competitiveness, for facing the reality of failure in life, by taking us out after a loss. To them I say, "Lighten up." Losing a soccer game does not equate to being fired from a job or losing your home. I feel as though kids ought to be given a little more credit. I don't think anyone on our team actually thought that having pizza meant we had *won* the game. I for one felt horrible every time we lost. You know what cheered me up though? *Pizza.* Slice upon slice of pizza, served hot out of the oven.

Chapter 6: Sunday Mornings

Every Sunday morning, I found myself reminiscing about Saturday's game. Which play I made to deceive this player or that, which play I could have made better, which goal let in by our team might have been my fault in some way, and how I would remedy this in the next game, were all thoughts that ran through my mind.

However, I couldn't fully concentrate. Someone's voice kept interrupting my inward conversation. Before I knew it, I had lost focus altogether, and was forced to turn my gaze up to a pulpit, where our pastor was starting her sermon. She spoke of something Jesus said in a complicated diction I didn't understand.

"This is so boring," I thought. The 1889 mahogany wood bench was just as uncomfortable as it was last week, and the service was just as long. Actually, the service might have been a little longer than last week...

Either way, Sunday morning needed to be over. Now. The clock needed to hit 12:15, and we needed to stand up and go home. However, I would not tell anyone that I felt this way. No, I would sit here on this long wooden bench, pretend to listen intently, and sing every hymn asked of the congregation—and I would sing them well, too.

My heart, however, just wasn't in it, a fact that I hid fairly well from Mary and Janet, who applauded my attentiveness and recounting of parts of the sermon as great strides forward in my growing maturity. They were right in one sense, I guess: I was getting better and better at lying about my true emotions, something adults do on a daily basis.

To their credit, though, Janet and Mary never forced me to say anything positive or negative regarding religion. They always invited me to think for myself and draw my own conclusions from what I learned.

Our church, Takoma Park Presbyterian, encouraged open mindedness as well. Outside the old gray stone building there was a quote from Dr. King on a sign in front of the church that read, "Let justice roll down like waters, and righteousness like an everlasting stream."

The church considered itself to be a safe haven for peoples of all different ethnicities, creeds, and sexualities. The majority of the congregation was white, with a few African-American and Asian families sprinkled into the mix. In addition, the church also had several African immigrant families.

In addition to racial diversity, Takoma Park Presbyterian had a few gay and lesbian members as well. The church itself was (and is) very liberal, but that did not apply to the Presbyterian Church as a whole.

In the traditional Presbyterian Church, women as well as gays were prevented, until recently, from being ordained as elders within the church. Today, women are allowed to be ordained as elders, but gays are still cast out, depending upon the congregation.

Takoma Park Presbyterian for its part had no issue ordaining gays as elders and proved it by ordaining Mary as one. She served on the board of the church and was charged with making decisions about the church's future.

All the same, several members of the church took issue with the fact that Mary, as well as several others, were even allowed to attend the church. An atmosphere of tolerance was preached, but was not always followed.

Janet recalled an occasion in which a woman refused to hold her hand during a prayer circle. Sunday service had just let out and a vote was to be held on whether or not to accept members of the gay, lesbian, and transgender community. At the end of the vote, the members held a prayer circle to close out the session. Janet dangled both hands out for her fellow members to hold in meditation. The woman to Janet's right refused to take her hand, placing her own hand on her thigh instead. Janet simply took the hand of the other woman next to her, prayed, and said goodbye to the other members of church as she always did. She confesses today that the woman's actions didn't exactly make her happy, but she never let her anger get the best of her. She went back to church the next week.

Given how liberal Takoma Park is, Janet's story was especially surprising to hear. The congregation was so welcoming of our family that I imagined bigoted views to be something looked upon poorly in all avenues of life throughout the area.

However, even in that liberal town 5 miles from the capital of the United States, homophobic attitudes were still prevalent in small pockets. Most churches in the area still didn't ordain gays, and some didn't acknowledge their membership at all.

At that point in time, not knowing that certain members of Takoma Presbyterian Church were homophobic was probably a good thing for me. If I *had* known, I imagine that I would have taken church even less seriously than I did. I would have begun to think that people didn't fully believe in the God they were praising. How could they, after all, if they were spending half their time judging others for being a different sexuality than theirs?

It was as if people were blocking out the specific part of their mind that challenged them to look beyond one particular passage and conceptualize an overarching message. To me, most people were going to church to chant uplifting hymns to make themselves feel good for attending worship. That was it. They were going to church every Sunday to fulfill a chore, which is why they needed to go home to relax and watch football after their hard work was done.

For me, doing a chore that paid zero dollars and involved sitting on an uncomfortable wooden bench for 2 hours was not a good enough reason to wake up early on a Sunday. But I went. I went not to feel guilty for not going, which is the same reason I imagined (and still imagine) many people do today. Millions upon millions of people attend their places of worship each week, month, or day because they simply feel that they are *supposed* to. That was my opinion when I was 7 years old, and that is my opinion today.

When I began to write this book, one of the first things I wrote was that naturally, attending worship just because you are supposed to, is worse in some ways than never picking up the Torah, Quran, Bible, or any other religious text in the first place. When your body is doing something out of obligation instead of passion, the analytical side of your mind can be completely wiped out without proper caution. However, this obligation can also show how dedicated you are to your religion, how much you love it. Still, it is important to remain open minded. You are reading the words, you are telling yourself what they translate to, and you are reciting them in prayer every day, but why? Why are you reciting them? Is it to show you believe? And if so, then what is it you believe? Every monotheistic religious text has translated the phrase "God is love" in some fashion, but then why do so many of his children discriminate?

When reading, do people build their own interpretations of the texts? Or are they simply following what their imam, pastor, or rabbi preaches in their sermons? Do people read the text knowing deep down that their God may not exist? Do they continue to believe in the text on the concept of faith? Does their faith help them come to the conclusion that their God exists based on the conclusions they have reached after dissecting the Scripture? Or do they simply believe that the Scripture is true because God is true?

I pass no judgment and have no answers to the questions I pose. I simply hope that people are asking themselves questions like these on a Monday or a Tuesday, on a Thursday or a Friday. I simply hope that people care enough to do so, because Lord knows, I didn't.

In fact, I recently realized that I was not bored in church because I didn't care about religion in general. I was simply bored. Bored because I didn't have the capacity at that time to grasp the Scripture I was reading. As a 7-year-old, I was hardly equipped to fully conceptualize what I was hearing and seeing on Sunday mornings.

Therefore, 5 years ago, was the first time I believe that I actually started reading the Bible in earnest. It took me days to get through 20 pages, because I would have to stop every other line to analyze what I had just read. I was reading to find out what each line meant in relation to the story, or the overall theme of that particular book, (e.g., Luke and John).

I didn't like everything I read. I thought that some parts painted women in a negative light, and that other parts painted God as an egotistical being. This was opposite to the infallible God that had been spoken of in the sermons I had heard throughout my childhood and adolescence. I was learning that *this* God punished those who didn't believe in him and made examples of those who defied him, spreading violence and destruction to towns that dared to question his merit.

I wasn't okay with that. I'm still not okay with that. Couldn't an infallible God think of another method besides violence to deal with his dissenters?

As I read further, I found out that apparently he could, which is why he sent Jesus to show people how to live. I began to reason that God was learning. God was learning to better deal with his creations. Because of this, it could be inferred that God himself realized the error of some of his ways, and fought to correct them. That was fine with me. It actually made more sense than an infallible being who had to destroy a different city every 1,000 years whose inhabitants acted up to set things right again.

The thought that God was in fact fallible in some way helped me to better understand some of the contradictions throughout the Bible. I decided to ignore the negative things I read. For example, I reasoned that it was not fair to ask someone to be non-judgmental, while telling them to avoid the leper with poor health in the same breath. However, other passages in the Bible helped me to navigate daily living, reminding me to be patient and forgiving in times I wanted to lash out.

In many ways, my own interpretations of the Bible as a whole are contradictions as well. I choose to believe in the validity of the Bible, but only those parts I deem acceptable to my general viewpoint. I use the Bible for my own purposes, citing it only as a text that teaches me invaluable lessons.

The greatest minds in the world have done studies on why the Bible is historical fact; however, it was still written by people. Therefore, I take all of its messages with a grain of salt. This once again is where faith comes in. I do not have faith in every person who transcribed the Scriptures; therefore I do not fully believe that there is a God, and that his teachings are law. I do not believe that God does not exist, either. There is not enough evidence for me (Big Bang Theory, notwithstanding) that God does not exist, because that would require my full faith in science, which I do not possess either. When broken down, science is theory, and theory can be disproved. Theory is not an opinion; it is based on many levels of science to make it fact. However, facts change over time. For years science defined what made a planet by a distinctive set of parameters. Over time that definition changed, which led to Pluto no longer being defined as a planet. Even science can change. Propositions remain which are used to explain some aspect of the natural world that have remained intact for decades such as Einstein's Theory of Relativity, but not every theory holds up to that level of scrutiny.

So what do I believe? Does the child with two moms believe in anything? Well—yes. In truth, I believe in just about everything. I believe in God, I believe in science, I believe in evolution, I believe in intelligent design. Some may say that Evolution and intelligent design cannot coexist. I believe they can. If God intelligently created the universe, I see no reason why he (or she) could not create evolution as well.

I believe humans were blessed. I believe in chance. I believe in the existence of Jesus on Earth. I believe our time on Earth has an expiration date. I believe in the afterlife.

I also believe that the wise individual believes in many things, but admits that he truly knows nothing. There are some things that I believe in more strongly than others, but I try to abide by that motto as much as possible. Our society makes it seem as though there are those who believe in God and those who do not—those who ascribe to religion and those who do not. But there are millions of people out there just like me who embrace neither class of thought. In religious circles, we are often called atheists or agnostic (people who believe in a higher power). In non-religious circles, we are often called closeted Christians, or closeted Muslims, or closeted Jews. There is this need to put us in a box; to define what we believe. This is impossible, because half the time we are not sure where we fit ourselves. We just meld—however we feel, seeking more knowledge, looking to empower ourselves. People like us, people on a similar journey, come in all shapes, sizes, and colors. We are not defined by sexuality, race, or class in the same way that a Christian is not defined by those parameters, either. Being gay does not mean that you can't be a devoted Christian. And being straight does not mean you will follow Christ.

My two moms grew up in religious households. Mary was raised in an Irish Catholic home and Janet in a Polish Presbyterian one. Even though Janet disagreed with some of the practices of organized religion, she continued to go to church every Sunday because she felt it would be a good foundation for me. It was not until I was in my mid-teens that she decided that playing soccer every Sunday morning with my neighborhood team was an acceptable substitute, and even then, we made our way to church every other Sunday during the offseason. She never stopped teaching me to believe in the positive things I read and heard every Sunday morning.

Mary was living proof that being gay is not a sign that someone has not taken God into their life. She was kicked out of her Catholic church in her early 20s, when someone told a deacon within the church that she was gay. Despite the church's denial, she continued to have faith. When she was a member of Takoma Park Presbyterian, she organized an adult Bible group, which met at our house from time to time. In the evenings, she attended seminary classes in hopes of being ordained as a minister. The Presbyterian Church did not ordain gays and lesbians as ministers, but Mary hoped that the tide would change one day. She was right. She was right about a lot of things—much of which she would have told you was because of her faith. She described it this way in June of 1997:

> *"I've always felt close to God. Sometimes, I feel a tremendous communion and love with God. Sometimes, I'm so angry with God. Sometimes, I'm so angry with God my prayers are a string of curses. At the worst moments of my life, I've even doubted God. But*

mostly, God is simply with me, in the good, the bad and the indifferent. Our relationship

has had its ups and downs but is the single longest, sustaining relationship of my life.

God gave me strength and reassurance when I came to terms with my sexual

orientation; God endured a 5-year, highly publicized, notorious custody case with me.

Now I'm wondering whether or not God hates me."

It was funny, reading this. Because in spite of her doubts, in spite of how she felt, Mary still continued to go to seminary. I was there. Every night she came back into the house energized by a particular Bible verse. Every night she was able to complete a biblical project she was working on. Every night she went, she seemed at peace. Like she knew what her passion was. She, along with Janet, is the person who taught me what faith really is. She believed in something when it appeared as though she should not. When it appeared as though she should just give up on God, she just kept going. She believed that things would get better. And when they did not, she blamed God, but she kept serving him. She inspired me, and so I prayed every night. When she was sick, I prayed for her to get better every single night, even when I was not sure if God existed, I prayed.

Faith does not care whether or not you are gay. Faith does not care whether or not you have cancer. Faith does not care whether or not you are scared. Faith only cares that you try every day to have it. And some days you surprise even yourself.

I draw my own conclusions, and love others, regardless of what their positions on same-sex marriage and homosexuality may be. It has helped me to understand others who believe that my moms live a lifestyle that is immoral. It was hard to understand at first, but I grew to realize that their opinion lay not in hatred, but in their own interpretation of God's word. I would never understand why God would condemn a good person based upon who they loved, and they would never understand why someone would continue to be gay knowing that the Scripture condemned it. What was important for both of us to understand was that the Bible commanded us to love each other despite our differences.

Takoma Park Presbyterian preached this message and helped to foster an environment in which lessons of peaceful interaction remained the focal point of discussion. The same could be said for the elementary school I would soon attend.

Chapter 7: Quaker School

By the fall of 1994, I had graduated from the ranks of preschool and was now fit for the big leagues of elementary school. Friends Community School, located in College Park, Maryland, would be the institution that housed this change. It was a small private school that enrolled around 120 students in grades K-6. Mary and Janet decided that it would be a good fit for me after learning of the small class sizes and the hands-on teaching methods offered. Unfortunately, Devin and Pat did not attend Friends Community School, enrolling in Carole Highlands, a public school located up the street from us.

I wondered why I didn't attend that school as well, and why I wasn't considered "normal" enough to go to what I considered to be a regular institution.

I had no idea that Mary and Janet had carefully chosen Friends Community School after a long and arduous search. A few weeks before school started, they had arrived at a dead end and were about to send me to Carole Highlands, at which time Laurie, Devin and Pat's mom, suggested that they check out "this Quaker School" in College Park. It was said to be very accepting of all family types, and placed emphasis on a concept called "conflict resolution," which the Quakers prided themselves on teaching. Mary and Janet were satisfied with the general philosophy of the school, and moved forward with the enrollment process. And so began my introduction to what I came to know simply as "FCS."

I do not recall that first day of school, but I do remember feeling like a big kid. I was spending more time away from my parents than I ever had, which gave me a sense of independence. Having a lot of fun at school didn't hurt either. Almost all of my memories from that first year at FCS place me somewhere outside, playing on the jungle gym or kicking a soccer ball around. I learned things in class, but all that transpired within the classroom served as a mere backdrop to the changing scene that was my kindergarten experience.

Much of that experience included learning about the Quaker way of life. Quakers are a Christian denomination that believes in nonviolent conflict resolution. Under this belief, all forms of war and capital punishment are immoral. Quakers refuse to participate in wars, and can be excused from military duty by informing the U.S. Government that they are conscientious objectors. (Non-Quakers may do this as well, but need documentation affirming that they are conscientious objectors.)

FCS took great care to make sure their students understood the importance of nonviolent conflict resolution, and held weekly exercises designed to teach us and test our knowledge of the practice. The exercises focused on using "I feel" statements to express how you are feeling to others who have upset you in some way. For example, if a child takes your ball on the playground, you would go up to him or her and say "I feel hurt when you took the ball, because I thought it was for everyone to share. I would feel better if all of us shared the ball, so we could all enjoy playing basketball." The other person would reply using an "I feel" statement as well—it might go something like this: "I feel left out, because you and your friend used the ball this whole time. I wanted to use it, too, and feel everyone should be included."
From this point on, both parties would be able to "place themselves in the others' shoes" as Quakers say, and find a solution that works for everyone.

One day, I asked a boy for my ball back using an "I feel" statement. He looked at me, looked around the gym, then dropped the ball. I smiled in a welcoming way, on the verge of thanking him. He looked me dead in the eye, then wound his shoulder back before punching me in the gut. He knelt down, picked up the ball, and went to the other end of the court. I clutched my stomach, wondering why the Quakers had lied to me about the world around me. They had not lied to me, though, the simple fact was just that not everybody in the world embraced their values. I learned that day that for everyone, not every lesson was teachable, and that it might be a good idea for me to learn how to fight a little better.

Still, finding amicable solutions for all parties was something that I still wanted. For that, I was grateful to have FCS. Responding to conflicts with well-thought-out responses was continually stressful. Its essence was "treat others as you want to be treated," which was the slogan reinforced over and over throughout the day. Every time some kids had an argument over whose Legos were whose, the teacher would stress this very slogan. It usually worked.

The Quaker way of life began to rub off onto me, too. I listened to the nonviolent lessons, and started to understand the power of conflict resolution.

I read up on the nonviolent movements of Gandhi and Martin Luther King, Jr., and was continually amazed at the changes they were able to make by turning the other cheek when hatred attempted to break them down, or worse, threatened their lives.

Daily worship sessions helped to drive this point home for me. Every day after lunch, the class would gather to take part in "worship sharing," a practice common within the Quaker community.

During worship sharing, a group of people convene for what has often been called a type of "guided meditation." During this time, the selected leader (in this case, a teacher) defines a question as the focus for sharing that is simple, open ended, and oriented toward individual experience. It might be a question about the spiritual journey, such as "How do you feel your spirituality has changed over time?", or one specific to current events: "What do I long for most in our community?"

During worship, all in attendance sit silently in a semi-circle for at least 30 minutes. Throughout this time, all who have thoughts and feelings on the question under study are encouraged to speak out of the silence. Between speakers, a brief period of silence is observed, at which time the next speaker is free to share his or her thoughts as well. The speaker does not respond to what anyone else has said, either to praise or dispute it. Each person is allowed to speak only once, until everyone has had a chance to speak. An object is often passed around to each person who wishes to speak. For instance, something as elementary as a stick may be used in this manner.

When someone does not wish to speak, they have the option of "passing" and handing the object along to the next person. Each person who speaks is asked to do so from their own experience, and concentrate on feelings and changes rather than opinions and theories. In addition to this, full confidentiality is respected with regard to all that is shared within the circle.

When I was at FCS, I heard several personal stories during worship involving family conflicts and issues. In each of these cases, the respondent observed worship to be a therapeutic experience for them. That semi-circle became a stress-relieving engine that asked for nothing in return. Since no one responded directly to their problems, they were able to express their feelings without fear of judgment.

For me, worship was a time for relaxation. My shoulders slackened, my eyes closed, and my body found the most comfortable sitting position available to it in that cramped space. My eyes would slip open and closed, carefully observing whether or the teacher noticed my antics. When her eyes failed to glance in my direction, I was free to drift off for a few short minutes.

However, most of the time I didn't drift too far from reality. My only goal was to clear my mind of all thoughts, which became impossible, and particularly implausible, in a cramped classroom. Frustration soon set in, at which point I attempted to fall asleep. When those efforts failed, boredom set in. It was only at this point that I looked at my fellow classmates to play a guessing game with their emotions. "Were they sad? Angered by something? Anxious? Bored?"

I yearned to find out, if only to kill the last 15 minutes of meeting. Unfortunately, this game proved boring as well. Most of my classmates appeared even more bored than I was.

However, there were times when their faces suggested more complicated thought processes. Their chins were clenched, their eyes closed, and their lips pursed in what could only be described as behaviors of people attempting to reach deep within themselves. I had no idea what each person was thinking, but I could tell whatever subject they were focusing on held great importance to them. Seeing this every day was humbling. It helped me realize that everyone has a different story, and different hardships to deal with on a daily basis. I felt foolish for spending so much time agonizing over my own issues, when others in my very classroom were facing equally daunting tasks.

Indeed, each time I learned of an elementary schoolmate's difficult predicament, I tried to treat them as I would want to be treated. I let them know that I would be there for them when they needed to talk, but that I'd also be there in the times they didn't —those times when they just wanted to play soccer, talk about girls, or recount Chicago Bulls games. I would be the friend for whatever the situation called for, brightening up their day in any way possible.

Chapter 8: Understanding Difference

Despite coming from a different familial background, I rarely felt out of place at my mostly white, Quaker, elementary school. I was never teased for having two moms or ostracized for having a different skin complexion than my parents. People often came up to me and asked why I had two moms, but their queries often seemed based in fascination rather than contempt.

There are over a million kids growing up in same-sex households, but that in no way means that other kids are aware of this. It can be easy to mistake a same-sex-headed household for another family type, especially if the same-sex parents happen to be of the same race as the child. They can simply be an aunt and a mom, or a mom and a friend. Or two committed heterosexual foster parents. The list goes on.

Does that kid have two moms? Are those his real parents? Are common thoughts someone who sees a child with two same-sex parents may think. It might be why their eyes look glazed over when they stare at same-sex-headed households in public. It may be why they show a second of hesitation before moving on to the next visual object. It might be why they pause on their way to the counter to examine faces of a family that is suddenly foreign.

For those around our family, those pauses seemed constant. On top of being a same-sex-headed family, we were a transracial one, as well. I could see it on the faces of waitresses, patrons, and passersby every time we went out. *Is that their son? Are those two women together? Where did they adopt him from (I bet Africa, no one adopts black babies from America.)* It was everywhere because our family was nowhere. They had never seen something like us—and so they wanted to know more, they wanted to guess which box to put us in. Or maybe, they simply wanted to see a new box altogether. I could not blame them. I did the same thing. Whenever Mary, Janet, and I saw a transracial family, or a black girl with two dads, or a white boy with two moms, I wondered what they were, how their family had come to be, how happy they were. I felt pride for those families, pride that they were like mine, pride that they dared to be different. However, pride is not why I kept staring over Janet's shoulder to look at them. Pride is not what forced me to listen to their conversations to see how much the kids talked like the adults—it was curiosity. What I was seeing before me was so unlike what I was used to, so out of the norm, that I could not help myself. I just had to know. And that's who we are as human beings—creatures of habit. We need to weed out unfamiliar scenarios. We need to dissect them. We need to try to understand them. We need to protect ourselves from the unknown. Everyone takes the time to do it, to examine every environment; the only question is for how long. So I could not blame others for being as curious as I was about a family structure that was unfamiliar. And so when people were diligent enough to go beyond staring and ask the important questions, I tried to help them understand as best I could.

One blond-haired boy, for example, cornered me on the subject one day after school in third grade.

"So, do you have two moms?" He asked. "I mean—I see two different women picking you up all the time…" he added, trailing off.

"Actually, I have three." I replied.

"Three?" He said, his eyes widening.

"Yup," I said, "Mary, Janet, and my biological mother. Mary and Janet are my adoptive parents."

"So are they like your foster parents?" He asked slowly.

"They're actually my legal guardians, which is a little different," I said. "Foster parents don't have full parental rights and normally run a foster home and take care of multiple children. My moms only look after me."

I was wrong, legal guardians do not actually have all the same parental rights a biological parent has. They are not technically allowed to sanction doctor's visits or school enrollments unless they are deemed acceptable by someone with full parental rights. They are not entitled to rights of inheritance either, meaning that the state had no legal obligation to see that Mary's Social Security benefits went to me when she died.

However, on this day, I was unaware of all of those things. To me, Mary and Janet had been my legal guardians, my adoptive parents, my moms, since we plopped into each others' lives in 1992. The boy stood there thinking what I thought: that the two women who came to pick me up every day had the same parental rights as his mom and dad. He smiled then continued the conversation, a curious look in his eyes.

"Wow, man, that's really cool," he said. "Having three moms must be awesome."

"Yeah, man, it's pretty cool," I said with a smile.

"So do you still see your real mom?"

"No, I haven't seen her in a couple of years," I said, pausing.

"Oh, well I'm sorry to hear that, man."

"Yeah, thanks. She did the best she could. She's just sick and wasn't able to take care of me."

"Sorry to hear that," he said. "It's really cool that you have your adoptive parents to look after you though."

"Yeah, I know, man. A lot of kids aren't as lucky," I said.

"Yeah, that's true," he said.

"So, do your parents like, sleep in the same bed?" He asked with a nervous chuckle.

"Don't yours?" I replied with a genuine chuckle of my own.

"I mean, yeah they do, but you know…" he said, waiting for a response. "Is it, you know…weird, at all? Like, do you ever walk in on them?" He said as I continued to stare at him.

"Do I ever walk in on them sleeping?" I said with a hearty chuckle.

"No, I mean…"

"I'm just kidding; I understand what you mean," I said.

"It isn't weird at all honestly," I said. "I have never walked in on them, I mean I assume they do stuff when I'm asleep, like most parents do. They do kiss in front me though," I said shortly.

"Is that weird at all?" The boy asked inquisitively.

"No, not at all." I said.

"I've been raised by Janet and Mary my entire life really. They are my parents. So when they kiss in front of me, that's what I see. I don't see two women kissing or two lesbians, I just see Mary and Janet."

"There are times when I look away when they're kissing," I said as the boy looked on intently. "But that's because parents' kissing is gross," I said with another slight chuckle. "No kid wants to see their parents kissing. But in answer to your original question, no, it's not weird at all."

"Oh, okay," he said. "That's cool. So it's something that you don't really think about?" Something that's just normal?"

I paused. "Yes, it's just something that you don't think about. Obviously, I realize that I have two moms and look around and don't see many other kids with two moms, and realize that our family is different in that way. But with everything else we're exactly the same. I get grounded just like any other kid."

"Makes sense," he said. "I mean, if I hadn't seen Mary and Janet and you hadn't told me I would never have guessed you had two moms. You're a real normal guy, man, you were raised right. That's really cool though, I wish my life was that interesting," he said, both of us laughing now.

"Thanks." I said. "Everyone's life is interesting though, it's just looked at differently depending upon the situation."

"Yeah, that's true, but still, man… that's cool," he said, a smile on his face.

"Yeah, it is, thanks. Like I said, I was lucky."

We shook hands then said a few departing words before bidding each other goodbye, both of us less ignorant about the world than we were 30 minutes prior.

A few hours later I sat in my room, analyzing the conversation. I rolled over onto my side, replaying the sequence. Every question the boy asked had been fair. If I were in his shoes, I might have wondered the same things. I didn't like that he used the term "real mother" as if real and biological held the same definition, but I understood. Several people had asked about my "real" mother as well, as if Mary and Janet were mere stand-ins. I accepted that, to many people, they were. I also understood that to some, the only "real" parent of a child was the mother who birthed him/her and the father who made that birth possible. I also understood that people used the term "real mother" for lack of a better word. Adopted kids are all too familiar with the term "biological," but others may find it harder to find the term when describing a parental relationship. For this reason, I cut the blond-haired boy some slack and focused on his other words, all of which were positive. He had had some questions he wanted answers to, but it was obvious he respected me, and respected my moms. I had no idea what his parents believed in, but from our conversation I ascertained that he had been taught to think of all people with an open mind, which is all I could ask for.

Most people who asked questions of me were just like that boy, curious about a type of family they had never seen before. If kids and parents wanted to know about families like ours, the easiest way to effect policy on gay rights was simply to tell them. They needed to know that we were happy, that we were wholesome, that we were weird. They needed to know how much we loved each other.

Still, for our family, nothing seemed to be "easy." Drama always seemed present—invading our lives. At the time I thought our constant hardships were a byproduct of our family makeup; that kids with "normal" families simply went about their business without a care in the world. However, over time I learned that every family whether they were rich, black, white, poor, two parent, one parent or something else each have their own hardships. Friends who appeared to have "normal" nuclear families ended up facing more trials than I could imagine. Their problems were equally daunting, and left them with plenty of battle scars of their own. Eventually I realized that I did not have it harder than they did. My experiences were simply different, "unique," if you will, a fact I would discover soon enough.

Chapter 9: Custody

Her house was located in Northeast Washington, D.C., 30-35 minutes from my medium-sized suburban home in Takoma Park. I always hoped that something drastic would happen to cancel my visit, but nothing ever did. Saturday would come, the sun would rise in the morning. I would saunter around the house before plopping myself in front of our battle-worn black TV to watch my beloved cartoons. I lifted the clunky remote, turning the volume down a few notches so my moms didn't wake up, before turning to Channel 50. My mind zoned in and out, transfixed by the *Rugrats* show onscreen.

My 7-year old ears heard rumbling upstairs, meaning either Mary or Janet had woken from their slumber. Janet must have lost the coin toss this morning, because it was she who appeared in the doorway to ask me what I wanted for breakfast. "Pancakes, please," I said lazily.

"Okay, sweetie," Janet would say to her spoiled son, darting off to the kitchen. In a few minutes, sounds of cooking emerged, with the contents of a frying pan wafting a heavenly scent into the next room. Hunger engulfed me, diverting my attention. Ten long minutes passed before Janet's voice cut through the air, beckoning me to come collect what was rightfully mine. "Thanks, Mom," I said, before wolfing down my meal.

"You're welcome," she said cheerfully, passing me a glass of orange juice.

"We're leaving in a few minutes, so go ahead and finish your breakfast and take a shower," she said, closing the cabinet drawer. Anger and dread crossed paths in one moment, dampening my post-meal happiness.

"Okay," I said, scraping pancake crumbs into the trash before placing my plate in the sink. I walked upstairs and shuffled into an empty bathroom, undressing before trudging into the shower, a forlorn expression on my face. I turned the faucet on, letting the warm water soothe my body. I caressed my shoulders and back, enjoying my last few minutes of freedom.

Fifteen minutes later, I was fully dressed, awaiting my fate.

"Tony! Time to go!" Mary shouted in a tone that sounded somber to me. I muddled downstairs, putting on my coat and opening the door before Mary could get to it. Janet turned to Mary before closing the door behind us. It slammed shut, and we were off to the war zone once again.

Mary's small, red car shook as we crossed into the rocky Washington, D.C. streets. We always passed a church, but I never asked the name—I was silent for most of the car rides, uttering only, "So when are you picking me up?" at the beginning of each ride.

I would sit alone with my thoughts instead, counting down the minutes. The Cathedral came into focus, 15 minutes out. We passed the Pizza Hut, 8 minutes out. We rolled past Lincoln Street, 5 minutes out. We made a left into a neighborhood, 2 minutes out. We made a right before coming to a small hill, 1 minute out. We made a left as a short silver fence stared at us in the rearview mirror—30 seconds out. We drove past one townhouse, then two, then three—0 seconds out.

Grandma's old, red townhouse came into focus. I stared up at the closed blinds on the second floor. Mary and Janet twisted their necks to look into the backseat. "Okay, sweetie, we'll see you tomorrow," they said, contorting their bodies awkwardly to hug me with their seatbelts still on. "Have a good time," they added as I opened the door. I nodded curtly, closing the door gently, before turning around. I took a deep breath before walking toward the shiny, grey fence.

I took ten steps before arriving at an open gate, its hinges creaked eerily. I carefully locked it as metal clanged against metal. I walked up to the door slowly, taking care not to trip as I stepped on the gold "Welcome" mat. I paused briefly before rapping on the door twice. Silence, then footsteps. A greeting — "Hey, Tony!" as I stumbled inside; one brown hand stuck out, shaking my hand firmly.

"Hey," I said sheepishly, moving forward.

I hung up my jacket, which already smelled of smoke. My grandmother loved her cigarettes, and they burned 24/7. I made my way over to the side of the plastic covered table, where one of my uncles greeted me. Grandma sat at the end of the circular table, waiting for me to make a motion towards her. On most occasions, she greeted me with only a look. This look said, "So, you decided to show up." I guess she knew that I didn't particularly like coming there. Even so, she would make sure to ask questions about how I was.

"How you doin', baby?" she would say in her raspy voice.

"I'm good," I would reply timidly, too shy to ask how she was. "They watchin' the game over there," she would say— the signal for me to go to the TV room to watch the sporting event with my uncles. I sat down on the plastic-covered couch and my butt squeaked awkwardly. Usually there was one uncle there. He would greet me with a "What's up?" as I took my place on the sofa. I dreaded going to that sofa. I hated that sofa, not because of how it looked but because of what it represented. Here I was, a 7-year-old child, taken away from the only family he had known, and forced to sit on this couch for 3 hours with someone I barely knew. I sat on that couch for hours watching a football game. I hated the football game. Why couldn't we watch cartoons or *Saved by the Bell*? I hated this game. My uncle rarely made any remarks. He was either too interested in the football game or just didn't care about trying to connect with someone 20 years his junior during his football time.

"Thure's a asum—kist oda in da fridge!" My grandmother said during the commercial breaks. I often found it hard to understand her the first time, her baritone voice muffled by the sounds of coughing. Nevertheless, I was quick to get up, relishing an opportunity to get off of the couch for a second. I walked to the back and grabbed my orange soda. I sipped it, withdrawing my mouth from the can quickly. For some reason it tasted funny, as if there was some pulp in it. I hid a cringe and started toward the couch before spotting my grandmother, who waved me back over to the table. I stopped, walked to my left, and sat down with her. She paused and spoke clearly, aware that I would not speak up if I didn't understand her. "How do those people treat you?" she asked inquisitively.

I always responded with the same elementary answer. "They treat me nice," I would say. My grandmother grunted in a tone I imagined to connote skepticism, before shifting her body away from mine and taking another drag, signaling the end of the conversation.

She was a mercurial woman, one who dealt in statements rather than asking straightforward questions.

Some of her greatest hits:

"You know they wouldn't let us see you, though."

"So you know they took you from us."

"You know they don't let you have any black friends."

I always defended my moms, asserting how nice they were, but none of it seemed to quell Grandma's suspicions. I don't know if she was testing me to see if I would stand up for my moms, trying to a get a quote to use against them, or simply ribbing me. We both knew I didn't like going there, which certainly fueled her ire. Her own flesh and blood was hesitant to see his own grandmother, but wanted to run home to two people who wouldn't recognize his baby pictures if they saw them in a lineup. Her angst was understandable, but didn't change how I felt about spending time there. I still hated it, and wanted to leave as soon as possible.

Nights when I was obligated to stay over were especially difficult. The sun would fall and it would dawn upon me that Mary and Janet were not coming. I retreated to the unoccupied bedroom upstairs, setting my belongings down on the desk adjacent to the bed, before plopping on the mattress, observing my surroundings. There was no night light, and the street lights reflected eerily into the silent room. I remember sitting there with my eyes wide open, watching the shady figures of the night come into the room, one by one, expanding and shrinking as the cars that moved past the pale desolate window distorted the light. My comforting teddy bear was not beside me, and neither one of my moms were there to tuck me in. At home, Mary and Janet would pitter-patter upstairs shortly before I slid into bed, their tennis shoes squeaking on the wooden floor. I remembered how excited I got waiting for the door to creak open, the faces of the two most important people in my life soon to greet me. Sometimes, I pretended to be asleep so they could tuck me in silently. It was a comforting feeling... the warm blanket caressing my body as Janet and Mary waddled into the room, kissing me on each cheek as I clutched my teddy bear, calmer than I had ever been. They would stand up slowly, then return to their room, closing the door lightly behind them as they left.

I would slink under my covers, happy, but longing for more. My moms had each other's company in the other room, but I was always by myself, and at my grandmother's, I felt more alone during the night than ever.

Every slumber at my grandmother's house was a struggle. I kept waking up and trying to figure out where I was. It always took a few seconds for me to realize that I was not in my own bed. I woke up, looking at the ceiling—there were no neon stars covering it, the plastic dinosaurs on my bureau were nowhere to be seen, the windowsill that would have been occupied by my shoddily made dream catcher was empty. The blue glow from my grandmother's TV reflected into the hallway, as flickering images appeared against the wall.

I closed my eyes, lost in my own thoughts. The judge wanted me to stay here for good, and my grandmother kept pushing, trying to force me to say who I wanted to live with, even when she I knew I didn't like it here. *"What if Mary and Janet never came back?" "What if I never get to go back to my house again?" What if this was reality, and my life with Mary and Janet was the dream?"* I kept asking myself these questions, making it even harder to sleep. I tossed and turned all night, trying to fight my way to dream world. The overhead fan purred loudly, annoying me. I finally resigned myself to the fact that sleep was not on its way. I needed to distract myself. I needed a story, and so I turned to the last time I had interacted with Colleen, my birth mother.

***

It was a Saturday, and I was once again off to see my grandmother. However, this time I was much more excited. My mother was supposed to be there, a woman who I had seen less than 10 times in the 5 years since my second birthday. Mary's red car pulled up to the townhouse once again as I stepped out of the car, anxious. "Say 'hi' to her for me," Mary said.

"Ok," I said, hugging her goodbye. I walked to the gate once more, opening and closing it forcefully before stepping up to the porch and ringing the doorbell. I prepared to wait but the door swung open immediately, casting a shadow as my grandmother stepped into the light. "How you doin', baybeh?" she said.

"Great," I replied, casting my eyes to the back of the room.

"Colleen!" Grandma said harshly. "Toneh here!" My eyes flashed once again to the back of the room as a heavyset woman with a soft face stood up.

"Ooooohh, Tooony," she said softly. "Come here."

I looked her over once more before walking towards her, angling my body for the perfect hug. To my surprise she started walking towards me as well, opening her arms before I arrived. We met each other in the middle of the carpet, embracing for much longer than I had expected. I latched on to her awkwardly, my pint size frame coming up to her chin. She smiled, then released me, gazing into my eyes. "It's nice to see you," she said softly.

"It's nice to see you too, Mom," I replied.

"How have you been?" she asked gently.

"I've been okay," I said hesitantly.

"How are Mary, and—Janet?" She asked.

"Yeah, those are their names," I answered cheerfully. "They're both fine. Mary says 'hi,'" I said.

"Oooh, that's so niiice," she said in her thick, Southern D.C. accent. "They have always been so niiice." She added, sitting down. "So how are you doing in school?" she asked.

"I'm doing well," I replied confidently.

"That's great, baby," she said softly. "I'm very glad to hear that." She turned to my grandmother slowly. "The food smells great, Grandma," she said.

"Thanks, sweetie," Grandma said. "So how do you like living with them?" my mother asked abruptly, turning to me.

"It's cool." I replied shyly. "They are nice."

"I am glad they are taking care of you," she said, her voice weaker than before. "I wanted to take care of you," she said. "But I couldn't at the time."

"I know you tried mom. It's okay," I said. "I understand."

"You were only supposed to be with them temporarily," Grandma chimed in. "Then they stole you from us. I was supposed to take care of you, and then give you back to your mother when she was ready, but they made sure I couldn't. They never wanted us to see you again."

I glanced at my mother, who looked as though she was about to cry. "Your mother was ready to take care of you, but they wouldn't let her," Grandma said forcefully. "But now you are old enough to make your own decisions."

My mother began to steady herself, pushing her chair closer to mine. She scooted forward, and then turned to me, tilting her head so that we were face to face. Her eyes bore into mine.

"Tony," she said shortly afterwards. "Would you like to come home with me? Or would you rather stay with them?" she said, her hand clasping my knee.

"I—I would rather stay with them," I said, sinking into my chair. Colleen bowed her head, putting both hands over her eyes.

"Look! Look at what you've done to your mother!" Grandma said, pointing at Colleen, who began to sob.

"I still love you, Mom," I said softly, placing a hand on her shoulder.

"Look at what you've done to her!" My grandmother repeated. "This is how you treat your own mother! She's your mother. She's the only one you *got*," she said angrily. I sat in my chair, unmoved, unwilling to look up.

"Look at her! Look at her!" My grandmother yelled. For the first time I obliged, forcing myself to stare at the face of the woman I had hurt. Her body shook steadily, both of her hands still covering her face as tears ran from her fingertips to the bottom of her palms. She reached for the Kleenex box by the TV, clumsily grabbing one of the last tissues out of the box, dabbing each eye lightly, her right hand still covering her face.

"I still love you," I said, patting her shoulder as she wept. "You will always be my mom."

"Thanks, baybeh," she said softly, removing the tissue from her face. "I would still like to see you," I said more forcefully, clenching her shoulder.

"He's been brainwashed by them," Grandma said crossly. "He's been brainwashed by those white folks."

"That's not true, Grandma," I said. "I love them, they have raised me for as long as I can remember, they are my family, too."

"It's okay, Tony," Colleen said.

"Mom, please don't cry," I said shrewdly, wiping her cheek as she continued to weep into her chest. I tried to get her to look up, to smile, but she just sat there, as depressed as ever. My grandmother's voice continued to rumble in the background, spouting off obscenities at Mary and Janet, at the failure of the court, at herself.

No words were said for the next half-hour as the three of us sat in the room, our eyes glancing from the TV, back to our hands, and back to the TV again. Tom Brokaw's voice ebbed in and out as Grandma flipped from channel to channel. As the day turned to evening she put the remote down, picking up a box of menthols on the table. She plucked a cigarette from the middle of the container then fumbled on the table for her lighter. After finding it under a spare napkin, she put the cancer to her lips and lit up, the smoke framing her face under a grey haze. She took a long drag and settled back into her chair, picking up the remote with vigor, aimlessly flipping through more channels.

After what felt like hours, my birth mother stood up, her eyes still puffy and red. "Come here, baby," she said quietly. I complied, rising out of my chair to meet her. She put her arm around my neck, coddling my chin. "It was nice seeing you, Tonnyy," she said in the sweetest voice.

"It was nice seeing you too, mom," I said shyly.

"I have to go now," she said sadly. "But I will be back, and hopefully we can spend more time together."

"Definitely," I said confidently. She walked to the door, stopping in place before embracing my grandma. They hugged passionately, and then with a wave, she was gone.

***

I flashed back to reality, staring at the blank, white wall, my mother's face fading slowly from view. *That was hardest thing I've ever had to do*, I told myself. *But I had to do it.* I flipped my pillow to the cold side and settled into that uncomfortable resting period somewhere between sleep and wakefulness, replaying everything. So much of this custody battle, so much of my life, centered on issues of race and sexuality. For me though, it was never about that. I didn't care that Janet and Mary were white, I did not care that they were gay. I knew Colleen didn't, either. However, the fact that she was constantly told that I was being brainwashed, and that white people were not letting me see her, could not have been the easiest thing to hear. Sometimes people try to downplay race as if it does not matter, but it does. That tension still exists, especially among older generations. As in so many cases, class also factors into the discussion. Janet and Mary came from middle- and upper-class backgrounds. Both had Ivy League educations. Both had good careers. Both had no kids.

My mother did not have that level of social and economic capital. She had three kids, did what she could economically, and was not able to go to college. She is the sweetest person in the world. But even the sweetest person in the world can feel insecure. Even the sweetest person in the world can feel as though they are vulnerable to more powerful people who can take away everything they hold dear, and Mary and Janet, as nice as they were, were still the people responsible for her not being able to see her son on a more regular basis.

They may have been gay, but in every other way, they fit into the power structure better than she did. They knew more people, they had more influence, and they were white. In America, the latter has sometimes been enough.

So often in the country's past, there have been stories of the white family being saviors to the impoverished, unintelligent, black child. My professor worried that my story would be like that when I first mentioned writing a memoir. I cannot fault my grandmother, her lawyers, or my mother, for having those suspicions as well. Colleen always felt like I was being granted this great life; that I had escaped any serious problems by going to live with this white family. She was happy for me, but may have felt as though she did not belong in my new world. Whether or not that may have been the case if I was adopted by an upper-class black family is hard to tell, but I have a feeling that many of the same tensions would exist. The middle- or upper-class black family could play the role of savior in the same manner. The privileges and advantages that the upper- or middle- class black family would enjoy would be similar to that of a white family with the same socio-economic background. However, one true thing was clear: the fact that Mary and Janet were white did not help.

Part of me realized that even at age seven. Part of me realized that there were still unspoken tensions about a white family "stealing" a black baby and using him or her for their own purposes. Part of me understood that some blacks thought white people should never adopt a black child. Part of me understood that they thought it was an insult to the black community to infer in any way that a black boy would be better off being raised by whites than growing up with black parents. Part of me understood that this was why my grandmother seemed so unhappy with my placement. Part of me realized that for Colleen, it would be hard to be friends with the family that raised her baby without her. Part of me realized that my two families would never be close. But that would not stop me from trying to get them to respect each other. It would not stop me from telling the truth, either, something I learned to value years earlier.

Chapter 10: Taliano's

Taliano's was the pizza parlor in old Takoma Park. Flanked by an ice cream shop and a battle-worn movie store, it was one of Takoma Park's quaint little nooks. Our family ate there on occasions both special and ordinary, on birthdays and after soccer games. Mary and I were fond of the pepperoni pizza, while Janet was keen on the vegetarian pie with mushrooms and olives.

In the winter of 1994, we nestled in a shiny, squeaky red booth by the front of the restaurant. Janet gave me a quarter so I could play my favorite Motown songs on the jukebox as Mary drank her Coke. When my moms wanted a moment to talk, they tossed a few spare quarters at me so I could go play arcade pinball as we waited for our drinks. I raced back to the table when my root beer arrived, spilling soda on my front as I gulped until nothing but ice was left clinking in the plastic cup. The second the last drop of soda seeped out, my mind began to envision the pizza. I hoped the crust would be thick but crispy; hot, but not searing. Janet talked about something but my mind was gone, on sabbatical until it was nourished. Five minutes later our waitress came out bearing gifts. I tried not to stare at her but failed as she carefully hunched over to set our pizza down on the table before standing to deliver a perky smile. "Anything else I can get you?" she asked casually.

"No, I think we're all right," Janet said pleasantly. The waitress smiled and walked away, her pony tail wagging back and forth as she made her way back to the counter.

I absentmindedly picked up a slice as she disappeared from view, burning my tongue on the sticky cheese. I inhaled shortly, grabbing my glass. I picked it up and tilted it downward, forgetting how fast I had drained it earlier. It took less than a second for me to remember my error. My eyes lit up and I began to sweat as I looked for something to cool my mouth. Mary and Janet looked on, amused, observing their son learning his lesson the hard way.

"Mmm! Mmm!" I said, motioning for their glasses widely. Mary smirked, then handed me her water. I snatched it away rudely, drinking until my tongue was colder than the ice on its roof.

"Better?" Mary said slyly as I looked up from my glass.

"Much," I replied tersely.

"Good," she said as I settled in. "Tony," she said as I dug in to the cooled pizza with vigor. "There is something we would like to ask you." I looked up at her, my mouth still half full. "Can we ask it?" she said inquisitively.

"Yusss" I said through pepperoni and cheese.

"How—would you feel about your last name being Hynes?" She said brightly.

"I think that would be pretty cool." I said, plucking a strand of cheese off my crust.

I turned to Janet. "Will you change your last name to Hynes too?" I said excitedly.

"No, no," Janet said, smiling. "My last name will remain Simons."

"Oh, okay," I said as I returned to my meal, glancing up periodically to find Janet and Mary looking at each other, beaming.

My eyes lingered on them for a few seconds, recording how happy both of their faces looked, before returning to a more important matter—finishing my pizza. I plowed through the rest of my pie at warp speed, but as fast as I ate Janet and Mary still managed to finish before me. By the time I shoveled down my last pepperoni they were sitting calmly, twiddling their thumbs. The waitress walked up with our check, placing it on the table. "Thank you," Janet said politely, glancing towards the check as the waitress smiled before walking to the table behind us.

"What's the damage?" Mary said inquisitively.

"Not too bad," Janet said, placing a twenty and a ten on the table. "We can leave the change for her tip," she added.

"Great," Mary said brightly.

"All right champ, you ready to go?" Janet said.

"Mmm hmm," I said confidently, climbing out of the side of the booth, my butt squeaking awkwardly. Mary and Janet looked at me, smiling as I stumbled out. I steadied myself and shuffled in between them.

"How'd you like your pizza?" Mary said.

"It was great," I said politely. "Thanks."

"You're welcome," Mary said genuinely.

I pushed the glass door open as we walked outside onto the sidewalk, a full stomach poking out from underneath my Bull's jacket and a smile framing my chubby cheeks. The violet sky framed my two moms as I glanced up at them, a content look in my eye. Neither of them brought up Mary's burning question again, because it no longer needed to be addressed. We were already a family.

Chapter 11: Adoption

The next few days were a hectic run of fortune for our family. I did not know it at the time, but the day I consented to being a member of the Hynes clan was the same day the courts had granted Mary and Janet legal guardianship over me. That evening, a few friends came to the house to congratulate us. Our pastor, my social worker, and a few of Mary's and Janet's friends drank soda as I shuttled through each room, hiding from the grownups. The gathering was fairly short, and by the time the nightly news started, they had all departed. I heaved a sigh of relief as the last grownup left the house and slipped into my PJs. I went upstairs and slipped under my covers, excited for what was to come. I had been told that I was going to be "baptized" in a few weeks, something I had never heard of, but it sounded frightening and exhilarating. Mary and Janet told me that all my friends would be there, and that some water would be poured over my head in front of everybody. After that point, I would be "officially something." Either way, it sounded like fun to me. I smiled, envisioning the faces, the robes, the bread, the small cups of grape juice. My belly gurgled as I fell asleep, hungry, but at peace.

Three weeks later it was time. I had eaten, showered, and gotten dressed. Now I looked at myself in the mirror, examining my get-up. I pulled the pin on the tie as close to my Adams apple as I could muster, doing my best James Bond impersonation. I buttoned the top button of my double-breasted junior grey suit, flinching as Mary came swinging into the room.

"Well, don't you look handsome!" She exclaimed proudly, kneeling down to tie my shoe. "Mmm hmm, there you go," she said as she made the last loop around my left foot.

"Thanks, mama," I said, glancing at her tattered jeans. "Mama?" I asked shyly.

"Yes?" Mary said pleasantly. "When are you going to change?"

"Oh." She said. "I'm not going to change."

Janet came into the room as my mouth opened, interjecting before I had a chance to respond. "Okay, champ, lets hit the road," she said tersely, flashing an annoyed glance at Mary's jeans before checking her watch anxiously, absentmindedly straightening the collar of her blue blouse before throwing on her grey suit jacket. Mary moved toward the door, straightening her wrinkled dark blue button-up shirt, rolling up her sleeves.

"All right, and we're off," she said, opening the door. "C'mon, champ," Janet said, beckoning me to follow her out of the door. I obliged as Mary stayed back to close the door behind us, her keys clanking as she took care to lock the top lock.

I smiled as I walked into the sunlight. Finally it was here—my day! I got into the backseat and buckled my seatbelt as Janet adjusted the rearview mirror. Finally satisfied, she smiled, putting the key in the ignition. The car whirred hesitantly as she started the engine, picking up steam as we raced out of the driveway and down the dry road. I sat back in my seat, closing my eyes. Flickers of light interrupted the darkness as the sun reflected off of the trees, schools, and streetlights we passed on our way. When the flickers stopped, I knew we had reached our destination. I opened my eyes, immediately blinded by the harsh sunlight. By the time everything came into focus others were getting out of their cars, walking up the church steps. Everyone had on their Sunday best, dozens of black and brown shoes gleaming in the sunlight. I took them all in before walking up the old, grey, cracked steps, hand in hand with Mary and Janet. We reached the top step and walked through a well-polished brown mahogany door, stumbling into a deacon who greeted us in front of the last row of pews.

"Congratulations," he said, pausing to give a soft handshake to Mary and Janet before kneeling down to look me in the eye. "Congratulations, little guy," he said, shaking my small hand gently.

"Thanks," I said shyly, eager to get to my seat. "You guys can take a seat in the front row now if you'd like," he said politely, reading my mind.

"Thanks," Mary said as we began to make our way to our seats.

"You're welcome; take care," the deacon said kindly, strolling off to greet more smiling faces. I followed his path then made one of my own, walking 50 paces ahead before sliding in next to an older couple seated directly below the pulpit. Both moms followed my lead, shuffling in between the couple to sit next to me. They fidgeted restlessly against the harsh wood before pulling out pamphlets located in a pocket on the bench. I followed their lead, clumsily picking up a yellow paper of my own. I lazily flipped through each page, examining what looked to be the day's agenda. Bored, I lowered my gaze, stuffing the pamphlet back in its place as I craned my neck sideways, examining each new face to come through the door.

Many of them were people I knew, some of them were people I knew well, and a few of them were people I did not know at all.

Devin and Pat sauntered in, looking confused as Dennis and his wife, Laurie, smiled and waved at my moms. My friend Allison, whom had stayed at St. Ann's with me for a while before being adopted herself, galloped in wearing a blue floral dress, flanked by her awestruck parents, who made their way up the stairs and into the upper level. Kevin, our kind, burly neighbor from down the street, came in wearing the bemused expression of someone who had not been to a church service in a while. He managed to flash a grin all the same, posting up against one of the last pews in the back before awkwardly trying to fit between a short married couple. Josh, my pre-school buddy, pattered in wearing a nice brown junior suit, a sharp bowl cut on his head, and a navy blue clip-on tie. Walking in directly behind him was Ariana, my pre-school crush, who wore a beautiful yellow dress embroidered with red roses. Blushing, I corked my head back around and stared at the brown bench, examining every water spot, scratched surface, and rough edge I could find. By the time I turned back around, Ariana had disappeared into the crowd. I sighed in relief, continuing to scan the rest of the church, which now boasted a much bigger crowd than it had 10 minutes ago. Row after row was occupied, stretching all the way back. I had never seen the church as full as it was today, even on Christmas Eve.

I sensed that the service would start soon. People were settling into their seats, the ubiquitous chatter coming to a lull. Our pastor stood at the pulpit, glancing at a few longhand notes she had made on a legal pad. She flipped a page loudly before putting her notepad in a small compartment in the stand. For the first time she gazed up, taking in her congregation. She examined each row as I had, clearly astonished at the number of people who had showed up, before inching closer to the mic.

"Good morning!" She said in a booming voice, her lips nearly touching the microphone.

"Good morning!" The congregation roared back. "Thank you!" She shouted enthusiastically. "You may now be seated," she said. The church fell silent for a second before erupting with a cacophony of sounds as benches rattling and scraping, babies fussing, and lungs exhaling. The pastor looked on patiently, waiting for each sound to die down before speaking again.

"Now," she said calmly. "Who is here for the adoption?" The entire congregation laughed as more than half of the people in attendance raised their hands. "Excellent," she said, smiling tightly. "Well thank you all for coming! She bellowed. "We have a packed house today!" She said, gesturing to the rafters. "This speaks volumes about the great community we have, as well the great family these three individuals have become. Mary and Janet have been wonderful parents to Tony, who continues to be a joy to us all," she said. "We have gathered here today to celebrate him, and to formally welcome him into our congregation. The first hymn we will sing today is a reflection of that openness, and one in which I hope you all will join along in singing with me."

She fell silent, delicately picking up her horn-rimmed glasses, before taking up her hymnal. Pages fluttered and rustled as people picked their books from under the seats, riffling through the pages to find the hymn before the song began. I picked up my book as the first chords rang out, pausing to look at the faces in the crowd. By the time I was done scanning, everyone had bowed their heads and buried their faces in their books. Trying to make up for lost time, I quickly opened the cover and began searching for the right place, randomly scanning the end, middle, and beginning of the book. Giving up, I cheated and looked at Mary's and Janet's page. Janet, who saw me struggling to see which page she was on, took pity upon me and invited me closer. I tiptoed over to her as she lowered the book to within eye sight of my 4'5" frame. "Here," she said, pointing at an early page in her book. "We are singing this one," she said.

"Thanks," I whispered as the piano grew louder.

"Jesus loves me! This I know/for-the-Bible-tells-me-so/Little ones to Him belong/They are weak, but he is strooonggg." The congregation sang off-key.

Mary sang passionately as I looked on, mouthing the wrong words to a song I didn't know. It seemed to drone on and on, the same three notes present in the entire piece. It wasn't until the last four bars that I finally picked up on some of the words. "*Yes, Jesus loves me, yes, Jesus loves me, yes, Jesus loves me, The Bible tells me soooo.*" I sang shallowly as the song came to an end. People clapped as the chords faded out, men rubbing their foreheads with napkins as women absentmindedly fanning their faces with pamphlets.

"You may be seated." Our pastor said again. Everyone obliged, sitting quietly as a litany of benches creaked.

"Thank you all for singing along with me today," she said. "Now, it is time for *Children's Corner.*" She said. "For any new members of our congregation, every Sunday, we ask the children to come up to the front and sit for a special activity or story that speaks directly to them. Today, Mary has volunteered to lead Children's Corner. We thank her for being gracious enough to do so, and invite all of the children up to the front at this time to take part."

A tide of little feet were heard shuffling from different parts of the church as they made their way to the front row, stumbling on patches of carpet as they inched closer to their destination. I turned sideways and saw 30 bodies closing in on my location. I climbed down off of the bench and took place on the carpet located a few from the pulpit, ready to welcome my peers, bracing to be trampled. Two boys came around the corner with great fervor and plopped on each side of me, brushing up against my knees as they knelt on the carpet expectantly. Mary looked on as two-dozen boys and girls made a line around them, digging their shoulders into one another to gain better positions. She paused briefly, before marching around two children and taking her place below the pulpit. The kids stood still and lurched forward, excited to hear what Mary had in store. She pulled up a brown stool and sat down nonchalantly, crossing her legs before clearing her throat.

"Eh hem," she said hoarsely. "So, once upon a time there were two brothers, one was named Abraham, and the other was named…"

I did not hear the rest of what she said, because I was not listening. From the time her speech started, I was bored. These kids must have thought they were getting a show, but I heard this woman every day at home, and she was more interesting there. Here, on this day, her tone was flat, her demeanor glib, her voice weak. I looked at my feet, waiting for her to be finished as several other kids around looked up at her earnestly, whether or not they looked on with intrigue or simple politeness, was hard to tell.

Five minutes later, Mary's story was finally over. Her closing remarks ending with "By the grace of Abraham," (or something like that, I'm guessing). The children stood up, shaking her hand as they walked by.

"Wasn't that a wonderful story from Mary?" Our pastor said rhetorically. Several heads nodded, smiling at Mary.

"Thanks, Tony's mom," one child said.

"Yeah, thanks," another child said curtly, making his way to the hallway as if a bathroom break was in order.

"You're welcome," Mary said, brushing off her faded jeans as Janet looked on disapprovingly.

"Okay!" The pastor said passionately. "If all of the kids would make their way to the hallway now it would be greatly appreciated." Hordes of swift feet obliged as the kids gathered where the bathroom-deprived boy had been moments before, huddling up by the staircase. Two adults slowly got up from their pews in the middle rows, meeting them by the top step. "All right, guys and gals," one of them said jovially. "Let's head on downstairs for Sunday lesson." Several kids smiled, glad to be free of the adults at last.

I watched them go down the small, winding, staircase without me, growing scared. In a few short minutes all eyes would be on me. I wasn't sure I was ready. I sauntered back to my seat, awaiting my fate. The pastor stood back at her pulpit, speaking of kindness. I zoned in and out as she mentioned how important it was to always listen to what others had to say, even if their views differed from your own. It was all very nice, but I was anxious to get to the main event.

Ten minutes later, my prayers were answered. Reverend Garnett closed her sermon out with an "Amen," and then took a few deep breaths.

"At this time, we would like to call the Hynes-Simons family to the front," she said. Janet and Mary stood up, motioning for me to do the same. I obeyed sheepishly, nervously urging my body upward. Chip, my friendly rotund godfather who vaguely resembled Santa Claus with his snow-white bushy beard, directed me forward.

"You can stand right…*here,*" he said as we made our way to an altar located under the pulpit. Mary and Janet stood on each side of me, my short frame sandwiched in between the two women. Reverend Garnett looked down at us and smiled, straightening her robe.

"Thank you all again for coming," she said dramatically. "Baptism," she said, pausing "is the right of any Presbyterian who wishes to be a member of the church. It is about starting fresh, and about cleansing the soul. We all have done things in the past that we are not proud of—things we wish we could take back," she said poignantly. "When the individual is baptized, he or she is forgiven of those wrongdoings and granted the beginning of a new life. Today, Tony begins that new life, one in which I am glad to be a part of," she said.

I looked at my moms, who smiled proudly. Reverend Garnett turned to them, a look of understanding in her expression. "And—by what name will you call this child," she proclaimed. "Anthony Martin," Janet said, puffing her chest out as she uttered what would become my first and middle name.

"Very well," Garnett said. "Chip, as Tony's godfather, will you ask the question?" Garnett asked.

"Yes," Chip replied patiently, opening his arms. "And to the congregation," he said loudly. "Will you support these parents…?"

"YES!" The congregation triumphantly replied. Chip gathered himself, and then spoke once more. "Will you support this child?"

"YES!" The congregation boomed back. Chip nodded then slouched, giving the floor to Reverend Garnett.

"Excellent," she said. "Tony, will you please come forward?" she said. I nodded as the congregation fell silent, taking three short steps to the altar. Seconds later, I met Reverend Garnett's gaze. "Today, you begin your new life," Garnett said firmly, looking me directly in the eyes.

I bowed as she picked up a shiny white goblet, bringing it to her chest. "In the name of the Holy Father," she said. "We baptize this child, *Anthony Martin*." She lifted her cup and then set the tip down in the basin, holding it there until the goblet was overflowing. She lifted it out seconds later, the overflowing contents splashing onto the floor. She gripped the handle tightly, balancing the cup as if it were a carton of eggs.

I continued to bow my head, my neck beginning to throb. My knees, which remained still for a long time, began to shake as the goblet made it safely out of the basin and dangerously close to where I stood. Suddenly the sleeve of Reverend Garnett's white robe was upon my neck, the cold goblet brushing against my skin. Its silver skin moved; wobbling, shaking, tilting, then dipping. I braced myself, expecting a flood to rain down on my forehead—I was greeted with a light stream instead. The cold water dropped slowly as Garnett had commanded it to, then landed on my head with a light splash. For a spilt second, everything was dark as I closed my eyes, the water washing over me. When I opened them a moment later a fuzzy woman stood above me, waving her arms up high.

"You are born anew!" She said proudly, smiling. The congregation erupted with applause, claps and cries ringing through the chapel. From the front row to the rafters, they stood, smiling as wide as their faces would allow. My moms came forward, hugging their Presbyterian son until he could no longer breathe.

"So proud of you," Janet said, kissing me on the cheek.

"Thanks," I said blandly, smiling in hopes of freeing myself.

"You did a wonderful job!" Mary said, holding me closer.

"Great," I said cheerfully, finally able to exhale as they released me.

I squared my body to face the pulpit where Reverend Garnett stood, a mix of happiness and relief in her eyes. "Okay!" she said merrily, addressing the throng. "At this time we will sing "We Shall Overcome," per Anthony's request. If you know the words, please sing along," she said quietly as the music began to play.

I shuffled in my seat then corked my head to look back into the crowd. The tone was happy, but powerful. Kevin, our burly neighbor, sung the song with passion, his chin quivering as he belted out the words, placing emphasis on each syllable:

"We shall overcoooome, we shall overcooooome, we shall overcoooome, we shall over-come, one daaaay. Deep in my heart, I do believe, that we shall overcoomee, soooome, daaaay."

His eyes were steady, full of emotion as his lungs continued to work in overdrive, his chest heaving. I looked at my moms, both of whom were excitedly beginning a march through the aisles as I followed along, giving a high five to a neighborhood couple along the way. We went from row to row, embracing, laughing, and celebrating with the people who had come to see our family. Throughout our march, "We Shall Overcome" spread through every pew in the house. I did not fully understand it at the time, but at that moment, people celebrated more than just a baptism. Yes, they had come to see me formally join a church. Yes, they had come to see us represented as a family within that church. However, they had come for another reason: *history.* Most of the people in attendance that day realized that they were witnessing it, that they were a part of it.

In 1994, it was rare for a same-sex household to adopt a child. It was almost unheard for that same household to adopt a black child. Our congregation knew this, and supported us anyway. More importantly, they supported the beginning of a movement, a movement that had begun decades before, and a movement that would continue to change the course of history decades later.

I was only four at the time, but some part of me realized that my baptism was about more than holy water and a new name. I realized that our family was different, that we didn't necessarily fit in with the rest of our peers. I understood that there were people who would dislike us, simply because of our uniqueness.

I understood that this was why that day was so important. My baptism, and the image it portrayed—a young adopted boy standing with his two moms—highlighted our differences. However, in that difference our greatness was highlighted as well. The packed crowd that showed up to support us, and the smiling faces that made us feel welcome, proved how important we were to our community. It proved that while we were unique, we were not alone. The people sang "We shall Overcome," with us with such passion, because it signified a moment in which they stopped caring about how different they were while recognizing how their differences bonded them with their fellow man. It was a moment in which they too became a member of the outcast, the member of the group that would overcome. Their acceptance of that status was an admission that in our church, God valued a loving community over everything else, and that our community was stronger for it. As we circled from pew to pew, I realized how strong our community bond really was, and that my moms were not the only adopted family I had.

After the baptism ceremony, our closest friends and acquaintances circled back to Chip's house for a celebration. I nestled in the den with a couple of friends and played board games while the grownups chatted about grownup things. Five paces away, Janet bragged about something I had said or done. The woman she was talking to abruptly leaped up and made her way over to me. "That is very impressive, young man!" She said, bending down to shake my hand.

"Thanks," I said with slight hesitation in my voice, imagining what I had done to impress her so.

"You should be a proud mom!" she said, turning back to Janet.

"I am," Janet said, smiling down at me. She looked me up and down once more, giving a warm look of approval before beckoning the other woman to join her by the croissants. I melted into the sofa as they walked away.

I flickered between sleep and wakefulness as tipsy adults bumped into me, shaking my hand on their way out. Janet, Mary, and I were the last ones to leave a few hours later, stopping in front of the back porch to thank Chip and his wife, Leah.

"Thanks again," Mary said as we stepped onto the soft, well-manicured lawn. "We really appreciate you organizing this event and arranging all of this delectable food," she added, biting into a chocolate strawberry.

"You're welcome," Leah said politely. "You are welcome over here anytime—as you know. Have a safe trip home."

"Thanks," Janet said, "take care. Tony, what do we say?" Janet said firmly, turning to me. I straightened my back and puffed out my chest.

"Thank you for having us," I said politely.

"Oh, well thank you for coming!" Chip said, his broad shoulders bending towards the grass as he looked me in the eye.

"Congrats again!" he said, plunging forward to envelop me in one of his legendary bear hugs. His white beard showered down on me as he let go brusquely, drawing himself back up to full height. He regarded Mary and Janet for a few seconds, before bringing up something else that was completely irrelevant to me.

Grownups always do this, I thought to myself. *How hard is it to just say goodbye and walk away without further conversation?* I gazed up at the over-eager old folks surrounding me. They each told two more jokes, then bid each other adieu, waving goodbye as we walked up the sidewalk towards our car. I opened the door clumsily and hopped in, resting my head on the cold window. Mary and Janet strapped in as the car sailed down the residential neighborhood, passing several Christmas gnomes on the way. I closed my eyes as the last jolly plastic face faded from view, cycling through the day's images. From the baptism to the party, lights and colors scribbled their way into focus, putting me in a trance. I soaked it all in, tired as could be.

When the car stopped in the driveway I rolled out of the backseat, tripping on my own feet as I walked up the sidewalk. Janet held my hand as I walked through our front door, letting it go when she realized how eager I was to get upstairs. I hurtled up the steps and rambled into my room, tumbling into bed. I rolled under the covers and tucked my teddy bear close to my chest, closing my eyes. The room faded from view as fast as the day had, and before I knew it I was asleep.

I slept in the next day, Mary bringing me eggs in bed. I smiled as she placed them by my lap before picking up a fork and digging in. Everything was going so well that it seemed to be too good to be true. I kept thinking that eventually, something would happen, and that the other shoe would finally drop. In the meantime though, I had eggs to finish eating.

Chapter 12: The Other Shoe

First grade happened to be a very eventful year. The summer held great memories, and the fall offered great promise. I was fairly well liked in school, and homework wasn't especially daunting. I would arrive home at 5:00 p.m. and have all of my homework done by 5:30 p.m., at which point I was racing out of the door to my next misadventure. Devin and Pat were usually at the center of it, their cross trainers flashing through their front lawn as they hurried to greet me. We slapped hands as one of us ran to the back porch to pick up a soccer ball, tossing it widely to whoever was closer. We all laughed as the ball hit the unassuming person in the face, leaving a dirt stain as it rolled down the person's shirt before hitting the floor. Whoever's turn it was to be the brunt of the joke wiped his front off as we took turns attempting to head the ball back and forth. The ball whizzed through the air until it grew too dark to see, at which point we rolled it by a couple of old plants in the backyard. Minutes later, I returned home for dinner, and soon thereafter I was sound asleep in my cozy bed.

Unfortunately though, a looming custody battle would make those peaceful slumbers harder to come by. The battle did not begin that year, nor did it end there. However, the events of that time stand as the most vivid photos of a war that would rage on for several years after its assumed expiration date; its origins dating back to 1992.

***

It was during that winter that Mary and Janet decided that I would be the new addition to the family. They had rented me out long enough, and wanted to make the arrangement official. My grandmother however, was not as keen on the idea. For years, she had played the part of den mother, taking in children whose parents were no longer able to look after them. She loved all her relatives, and did whatever she could to make their lives easier. However, she understood that some of them would not amount to all she had in mind for them. She understood that some of them would have kids and not be able to take care of them. She also understood that those kids needed a home—and that if she wanted to keep the family together, that home would have to be hers.

And so she had gone to work, cooking, bathing, and potty training as needed, her 60-something-year-old frame moving about the house with power and purpose, picking up a linen cloth, scrubbing down a soiled bed. It was thankless work, one which required a combination of love and obligation to complete. If it fazed her, she refused to show it. Rain or shine, sleet or snow, her expression was the same, gruff, piercing, devious. Whenever an intruder walked into the house, there she was, smiling with her eyes and clenching with her teeth, ready to fire off her latest soliloquy.

However, when she found out my mother was pregnant with her second child, it is hard to imagine that a jovial bone could be found in her body. She cherished Colleen, but knew the road ahead would be tough for her. My mother had trouble on a day-to-day basis, and was not in the best position to take care of herself, let alone another person. When she was at the top of her game, she was the sweetest, most caring person in the world. However, she suffered from schizo-affective disorder, a condition that made it nearly impossible for her to be there for her kids when they needed her. My sister had turned out just fine, and had been raised by my grandmother as well. From the time Angie was an infant, Grandma worked hard to mold her into the young woman she would become. My grandmother did all she could for Angie, but she was not young anymore, and was having a difficult time raising a soon-to-be adolescent girl. Angie was smart, headstrong, and outgoing, all good qualities, but those also made for clashes between the two women. Angie wanted to go out, to be seen, to learn. But Grandma wanted to remind her that she was not a woman yet, that she had not reached any of her goals, and that she never would if she kept on the same path. She reminded Angie when she was fat, yelled at her for looking at her funny. It was a thankless job, feeding and clothing an ungrateful teenager. Adding another life into the fold was not in the cards. But what other choice did she have?

My mother was too far gone, and my father was nowhere to be found. My sister was too young to care for me, and I was devoid of older brothers. My grandmother was the only one to take on the task, a fact she knew. She had dealt with situations like these for decades, and understood what to expect. Even when I was put in an orphanage, it was expected to be temporary. She was supposed to be the person clothing and feeding me, even if she had too many kids already living with her.

She had cared for me throughout the first year of my life, and was prepared to do it again whenever Colleen was ready to pick me up from the orphanage and drop me off at her house. It wasn't until she got a call from a social worker that she realized reality offered a different outcome.

The call came on her home phone, the one located on the dining room table. Grandma answered it, listening intently to the voice on the other end of the line. She took in the words and tried to wrap her head around the fact that, one: I would not be going home with Colleen; two: I was going be taken by someone outside of the family; three: that that someone was white; and four: that that someone was a lesbian. She must have needed a smoke; I couldn't blame her, it was a lot to take in at once. The mere fact that I was going to be raised by someone outside of the family would have been enough to raise her ire. However, the fact that those people were white must have been especially difficult to handle. To her, it was as if I was being taken away from two families: the extended one she had created over 40 years ago when she had had her first child, and the black community she had lived in since she was born. Her entire family had been born and raised in and around Washington, D.C., a black-populated area if ever one existed. They married within the black community, they ate the food of the black community, they spoke like other members of the black community, and they lived with other members of the black community.

Technically, I was not her blood. She was in legal terms my great step-aunt only, the aunt- in-law of my mother. However, she would not allow that to stop her. She was determined to win me back, whatever it took. To her, I was a member of the family all the same, and family fought for each other.

Still, aside from her familial obligations, there was, of course, another reason my grandmother disapproved of my potential adoptive parents. Indeed, the elephant in the room happened to be a lesbian as well.

* * *

The elephant confidently walked into the room surrounded by two lawyers, ready to shoot arrows at anyone who dared attack their possession. My grandmother did not have an arrow, but she did have a shotgun of a mouth, and was prepared to use it to keep her enemy at bay.

* * *

It is apparent that my grandmother was uncomfortable with the very prospect of a lesbian couple raising her extended family member from the start. She was a woman of God, a woman who had not missed a Sunday service in over 20 years. Her best outfits were the ones she wore to church. Her best meals were the ones she cooked for relatives after it. She read her

Bible from front to back, and knew some passages better than the preachers that spoke them. She believed homosexuality was a sin, and that offenders would go to Hell. Jesus had taught her to love her neighbor—to hate the sin, but love the sinner. But the thought of a lesbian couple gaining custody of a loved one, was too much. If gay people wanted to be gay on their own time, that was okay with her. She would not discriminate or hate someone because he or she were gay. In fact, years later, she would have a grandson who was gay whom she would love with all of her heart. That was different though, than allowing a gay couple to raise one of her own.

Loving the sinner was one thing, but letting the sinner raise a child near and dear to your heart was another. Raising that child in an environment with two gay parents was something else entirely. The trepidation she felt rested in large part on the assumption that I would be more open with my sexuality because it was accepted in the gay household, leading me to the same Hell that awaited my two moms. She feared that there would be nothing she could do to stop it. Above all, she feared that I would be raised in an environment with no morals—an environment in which God's laws held no relevance. She wanted me to be the best man I could be, but it was hard for her to see how that would come to pass in an environment where Christ was not put first.

She did not know the people who had volunteered to raise me, and had no way of knowing whether or not she could trust them. She may have inferred that a household willing to engage in homosexuality was one in which the immorality of shielding a child from parts of his biological family would never be visited. She may have feared that if she did not fight for me, these white, lesbian, foreign-cultured people would take me away for good—and never look back.

It was for this reason that she filed a challenge when she learned that Mary and Janet had been allowed to adopt me. She filed an appeal and was granted part of her wish. Mary and Janet's adoption of me was overturned. They would no longer be considered my adoptive parents. Instead, they would be my legal guardians. They would have legal guardianship of me, but would not be entitled to many of the same rights adoptive parents would have. As legal guardians, they were not entitled to put me in their wills as next of kin. This is important because when someone dies, their next of kin does not have to pay taxes on the estate of the deceased. When Mary died, Janet had to pay $20,000 in taxes on her estate because they were not married, and therefore she did not qualify as next of kin.

Other issues arose as a result of simple legal guardianship as well. In my case, when I needed a birth certificate for my learner's permit, I was unable to get it because Janet and Mary did not have the right to request my birth certificate as legal guardians, which became a problem. For instance, when my class went on a field trip to Canada in high school, I was unable to go because I could not secure a passport, because I had no official birth certificate with my name on it. I was unable to get a job before I turned 18 for the same reason. No one in Grandma's family knew where my birth certificate was, and because my name was legally Hynes, I was unable to claim that I had a right to the birth certificate of Tony Lee Jones, my name at birth. My name being changed, along with the judge's overturning of my adoption, had made it difficult for me to prove who I was. However, changing my name back would also be difficult, because all of my medical documents now had the name Anthony Hynes stamped on them. Janet admits that she and Mary did not imagine the name change would cause so much havoc. Had they known, it is possible that they would have declined to change my name to

Hynes. Still, if the adoption had held, none of that would have mattered: Mary and Janet would

have been able to request my birth certificate themselves as adoptive parents.

Thirteen years later, Janet would adopt me. I would be 19; 1 year older than the age

required to go forth with the adoption process without the courts notifying the biological family.

The proceeding would go smoothly in a court in Baltimore. We would be one of several same-

sex-headed households granted adoption that day, smiles and tears on our faces. She would

finally be able to put me in her will as her next of kin, and I would finally be able to get my

birth certificate, my learner's permit, and a passport.

However, in the interim, adoption was out of the question. For my grandmother,

knocking Mary and Janet down to legal guardians was okay, but obtaining full custody of me

was still the goal.

She procured a lawyer and a social worker, and then began to present a case she was

assured she would win. Her team went to work, sharpening its claws. They began the battle by

arguing that she was my closest next of kin, and for that reason alone should receive the court's

blessing to raise me. She argued that the biological family, if ready and willing, should always

have custody of the children in question, and that this instance was no different. Her lawyers

built their case on the testimony of doctors who echoed that sentiment by pulling from

numerous qualitative and quantitative studies showing how much better a child raised in his or

her biological home faired in relation to their familial estranged counterparts. The fact that she

was not my grandmother, but merely my step-great-aunt, was not mentioned—at first. My

grandmother swore up and down that she was my biological grandmother, and that she had

birthed Colleen. She was confident that when this fact was brought up, it would win her points

with the judge. Given past history, she had reason to believe it would. Much of the trends favored her. In matters of custody and legal guardianship, the biological family was normally granted custody. Her case would have ended up the same way—if she were able to keep up the ruse, that is. Instead, when the courts pressed harder, she was forced to produce papers documenting her true familial relationship to me. When it was proved that she was in fact my step-great-aunt and nothing more—the sister-in-law of my mother's mother—her challenge became substantially harder to win. Even though she was ready and willing to raise me, in the eyes of the law, she was merely another party interested in gaining legal guardianship.

Her challenge was doomed from the start, a fact she must have known early on. However, she still had a chance to gain the outcome she was looking for. There was a way for her to save me from the white folks and raise me, as well. All she needed was a couple of people willing to take up the challenge with her. It would not take long. Indeed, before she knew it, she had two people standing with her, ready to fight the good fight.

∎∎

One of those people was Colleen, whose lawyers made a challenge for custody of their own. From the outset, it was apparent that her case was stronger than my grandmother's. She was my biological mother, had claimed me at birth, and was willing to raise me. She had no criminal history, and had the financial means to raise me. Still, her case was weakened by two factors: the first being that she wanted my grandmother to raise me instead of her for the time being; and the second, was that she was schizophrenic. Those two factors alone made it a tough sell. When she failed to show up to a follow-up court summons, her case was made all but impossible. Why she failed to show up was never discovered, but it must have left the judge wondering whether or not she was responsible and lucid enough to be in my life, let alone raise me. She was dismissed as an applicant for custody of me within a week. I had no knowledge of this at the time, and would not know that my mother had failed to show up in court to claim me until I was in my early teens. It would not be until this time that I would wonder about the depths of my mother's illness. I had always known about it, but both families had done a good job shielding me from how sick my mother really was. My step-great- aunt only let Colleen see me when she was on her medication. The two legal guardians whom I called Mommy and Mom did the same, inviting Colleen over only when they knew she was taking her meds, sometimes with a social worker at her side.

Her condition, schizo-affective disorder, was not discussed. I would know nothing of her paranoid delusions, or of the time she believed a rat had chewed off her finger even when witnesses had seen her ding it on a lamp post.

Her life was not one safe for a child to see, or in which to be raised. However, when she was on her meds, she could manage just fine. And she did want to see me, to be there for me. However, she knew that she was not well enough to make that happen. Still, she had dreams of raising me by herself one day, prompting her to file the initial challenge.

The plan was always for my grandmother to take care of me until Colleen was better, at which point Colleen would take the reins. However, some part of Colleen must have known that her plan was a long shot. She had tried to do the same thing with my sister, who was nine years my senior. My sister got to see Colleen from time to time, but was never once raised by her. That duty fell to my grandmother, who took my sister in and raised her like a stepchild, as she had done with several other children. She was willing to take up the post once again in this case.

However, when Colleen failed to show up for court, those hopes were dashed. There was only one person now who could turn the tide in my grandmother's favor now, and she was not confident in the slightest about his chances of coming through.

Ch. 13: Making a Family

That person was Damon Lowe, my father. For the first time in his life, it appeared as though he wanted to be more than a sperm donor to his son. He had gotten wind of who would be raising me, and decided it was time to put his hat in the race. He and his lawyers made their challenge simultaneously with Colleen, in hopes of presenting a united front. I do not recall my father being in court, and do not even know what his face looks like. All I can ascertain is Janet's word and the language taken from the court documents. Both sources of information state that Damon Lowe and his lawyers presented a challenge to Mary and Janet becoming legal guardians on the grounds that "I would not be raised in a safe environment." Damon Lowe's lawyers were more blunt than my grandmother's, and relayed what Damon must have said himself to them behind closed doors.

Damon's challenge had something to do with him eventually wanting to see me, but was mostly based upon whom it was proposed would raise me. Damon simply did not want me raised by two women who were white and who were lesbians. It was as simple as that. His son would not be raised in that type of household if he had a say in the matter. He was fine with me living somewhere other than his own home, but wanted the home I would be raised in to be masculine, black, and strong. He viewed Mary and Janet, on face value, as exactly the opposite.

His challenge held more weight than Colleen's. He was my biological father, he was not seeking full custody, and he was lucid enough to stand trial. All he had to do was show up in court to claim me. Unfortunately, that something proved inexplicably difficult for him to manage. He did not show up the day his lawyers read out his challenge, and he did not show up again when summoned by a judge. Because of this, his challenge to gain custody failed to gain any significant traction, and was dismissed almost as soon as it had arrived. He may have felt that it was harmful for me to grow up in a home with two lesbians, but it was not enough to make him something he had not been a day in his life—reliable. I do not recall having any contact with him at that time, and I have no stories of us interacting during my first two-to-three years on earth. As was the case with Colleen, I had no idea that he was even one of the parties challenging Mary's and Janet's initial claim to obtain legal guardianship until years later.

That knowledge was neither disheartening nor stress inducing. I had always wanted a father, but I had never wanted *him*. Maybe someday that will change. But then, as now, I remained a young man who realized who his real family was.

The courts however, failed to realize that reality as readily. The battle that had started in the winter went into the summer, then into the fall. Social workers came to the house as lawyers walked out of it, explaining to Mary and Janet how to best proceed. No party stayed for longer than a few hours on a few lonely weekends a month, but their presence was felt long after their departure. "Social worker" became a dirty word, a code for the person that would take me away from my home if we lost. In between their comings and goings, I was slated to continue visiting my grandmother, who never missed an opportunity to influence my opinion on the case. She took great pride in making sure I realized that they had "stolen me" and that eventually I would come to live with her. Her talks normally ended with me feeling mad at her, rather than suspicious of Mary and Janet.

In and out of court we went, dancing around the topic of legal guardianship until my feet were sore. None of it seemed right or fair. Two sides fought for supremacy in a battle that had no clear winners or losers. Janet and Mary were tired—Grandma was, too. However, each party soldiered on. Mary and Janet argued that they offered a great home for me as my grandmother shouted her distaste for their parental qualifications. It was the same argument said a different way. They were gay; we got it. They should not be parents because of it; we got it. As time moved on, Grandma and her lawyers became more creative players, drawing on more potential angles to win the case. When they grew tired of insinuating that a lesbian home was a poor one in which to raise a child, they turned to a subject they felt would win them more points with the judge: race.

If continuously mentioning homosexuality threatened to make them look bigoted, the topic of race offered an opportunity to get back on common ground. It was less taboo, and more open for debate. Grandma's lawyers used this to their advantage, proclaiming that it was possibly racist, and factually irresponsible, to allow me to be raised by a white family when a willing black family was ready to fulfill that duty. *"Black families,"* they said, *"rarely adopted white kids, so why should white families be afforded the same opportunity?"*

"Children," they said, *"need to see themselves in their parents."*

"Black children raised in a white household," they said, *"grow up to be racially confused individuals. The lack of positive black role models the adopted black child raised in the white household has,"* they said, *"hinders their ability to embrace their cultural selves. Because they are unable to embrace their cultural selves, they are unable to realize themselves completely. Thus, an important piece of who they are will always be missing—they will never be whole. They will attempt to fill that hole with laughter, depression, or anger, but it will still be there."*

"The worst part," they said, *"is that because they are so unfit culturally, they will have no way of knowing why the hole is there in the first place."*

"In addition to this," they said, *"granting a white family custody of a black child subconsciously tells the child that it is the white household that is ideal, that the black household is less than desirable. "Sending me to live with a white family," it was said, "would reinforce this stereotype, and rob my mother and her family of proving it wrong."* To my grandmother's team, the decision should have been an easy one for the judge to make. It was simple—*being raised by white people would cut off my social and cultural ties to the African-American community. To prevent that, the judge needed to intervene and grant my grandmother full custody.*

It was an easy, plausible argument to make, and one that the judge had to consider. From where Mary and Janet sat, it was an undeniably short-sighted one. They viewed themselves as good people, people who would do right by their child. However, there was a part of them that remained anxious about the idea of raising a black child.

I had graduated from college by the time Janet was able to admit it. "We wondered whether white people could raise a black child," Janet said when I asked her if they worried about raising a black son.

"Before we met you, I talked to a woman at my work who was adopted by a white family," she said. "She told me that she would have rather not have been raised by a white family."

"Why did she say that?" I asked.

"Well," Janet said. "She said she felt deprived of her cultural heritage…" "*But,"* Janet continued. "We also talked to two black boys raised by white families at our church who said that they loved their household and had no problem being raised by whites. So, we had these conflicting reports."

"So how did you get over that?" I asked.

"Well, we spent time with you," she said in a matter of fact tone.

"And that was all you needed?" I asked.

"Well, yes." Janet said. "We found out through our bond with you that we would be fine. There wasn't anything else we needed to discuss," she said.

"In addition to that, our bond with the community of Takoma Park was also helpful," she said. "There were so many beautiful multiracial and multi-ethnic families—adding one more didn't seem like a stretch," she said. "On top of that, the community was very supportive of us," she said. "We had a lot of people come up to us saying that what we were doing was great."

"That's really good to hear," I said, putting down my pen. "Thanks, Mom," I added abruptly, running upstairs before she could get another word in.

"You're welcome!" I heard before hitting the top step. I paused before walking across the cold wood floor before stumbling into my room. I sat down on my bed, lunging to pick up my laptop, which sat atop an unopened printer case. I pushed a couple of old yearbook photos out of the way before rescuing it from its resting place. I clumsily held it with one hand, lazily putting it down on my bed before opening it. The white screen flashed in front of me, littered with the black letters that had coated yesterday's blank page. I clipped my headphones on, rocking out to one of my favorite Eminem songs, before beginning to type. The keyboard went "click clack," as I straightened my back, digging within myself to see the overall meaning in my mom's words.

It seemed to me as though she was admitting that some part of my Grandma was right to be scared about a white family raising me. All transracial adoption cases are different, and each presented a risk. If an African-American boy is adopted by a white family who fails to teach him about his cultural heritage, his future family's cultural history may die with him. Others kids, much like the woman Janet described, may grow up feeling as if they have been deprived of their cultural heritage. I did not see the woman who proposed her cultural heritage had been stolen from her, however, her words connoted that she felt as though her culture was something she had been denied. It was as if it was something available, but hidden from her, lest she become more "exotic" than her adoptive family intended. Whether the adoptive family did this intentionally or unintentionally was irrelevant. She grew up resenting them either way, robbed of a culture that could have been hers.

Her story, which was still playing itself out, was not the best for Mary's and Janet's case. On the contrary, her upbringing, and her subsequent resentment, would have made her a great witness for the opposition. From Janet's account she was smart, polite, and successful — a perfect confidant for my grandmother's team. Her adoptive family had obviously done a great job raising her, but still left their adopted daughter feeling as though she was missing something. If they had had the capacity to call her to the stand, grandma's lawyers would have had the chance to argue that her adoptive family was well meaning, but flawed—that they had the right amount of money and social capital to raise a healthy child—just not a black one.

Mary and Janet would have been forced to confront the reality that in this case, they were right. For whatever reason, the adoptive family of the young woman had not made her feel as though it was okay to explore her cultural heritage at length. Despite the fine woman she had become, that would always be true. She could enroll in the best college, marry the best doctor, and give birth to the healthiest baby, but a part of her would always feel like a failure. If the opposition had had a crack at her, they would have argued that she was damaged goods, that she was insecure because she felt as though it was her fault she had not done more to learn more about her culture growing up. They would argue that part of her would feel as though it was she who had shied away from her race—even though it was her parents. They would argue that if she had connected with a distinctive part of her culture sooner, she would not have harbored the anger and confusion that had become a part of her soul. They would argue that if she had been able to find out more about herself sooner, her young adult life would not have had to be one of constant soul searching, of rediscovery.

It would have been a worthy argument to make. Indeed, if the majority of transracial adoptive cases were like hers, it would be unwise to place a child of a different race in a household with people who did not look like him or her.

However, not every transracial case was like that of the young woman. On the contrary, there were many cases that had different endings than the story she had described. Several of them happened to come from people I knew. Allison, David, and Isaac were their names, and all of them had a distinctive story to tell. I was lucky enough to meet each at different stages in their lives: Allison in preschool. Isaac in middle school, and David in college. Each of them were eager to talk about their parents, and more open than I had hoped for.

Each was a different race than their adoptive parents: Isaac was Latino, Allison was black, and David was South Korean. All of their parents were white, first-time adoptive parents. I asked each about their experiences growing up, about where they were now, and how they felt about their adoptive parents. Isaac was first. He was always the talker, the showboat. I met him when we were nine, two eager soccer players at a summer camp in suburban Maryland ready to take on a whole team by ourselves. He talked trash to the other kids even when we were up by five or six goals, constantly reminding them how much better we were than them—I was not friends with him. If anything, I saw him as my rival, a more arrogant version of myself. High school would be the first time I saw him in shades of grey.

I remember being surprised on the first day of orientation when I saw him. "What's up, man!?" he had said boisterously. "Didn't know you went here!"

"Yeah, man!" I said, caught off guard by how happy he seemed to see me.

"You find out about this school through Ron, too?" He asked.

"Yeah," I said, "My mom and I ran into him and he suggested I check it out."

"Well, good!" Isaac said. "Now I have someone to play some soccer with," he said. "Was worried no one in this school liked sports."

"Yeah, you—were right to be worried," I said. "We should definitely do that though," I added. He nodded furiously as if readying himself for a challenge.

Within weeks we had become good friends, kicking the soccer ball around after school and talking about girls. Isaac would go on and on about his top five women. He always mentioned Megan Good, Serena Williams, and Lauren London (all black women). He would get this glint in his eye while describing them, tipping his hat to the side like his favorite rapper. It was funny, seeing him act in such a way. Here was a Columbian boy, adopted by a white family, fully embracing black culture. He did not associate with Latin-American culture, and spoke Spanish at a C- level at best. His parents were well-meaning, but never impressed upon me that they were worried about their son's cultural background. No Columbian dishes were cooked at the house, and no visits to Latin America were mentioned. They were just like every other family on their suburban block. Perhaps this is why Isaac felt the need to be so boisterous, to stand out.

Indeed, he did it at every level, from loud boasts about his soccer skills in high school, to talk of his club promoting skills in our late teens, to stories of his rendezvous with celebrities in our college years. He was a nice person, one of those human beings who you genuinely felt wanted the best for you at all times. However, I sometimes thought that he lacked in the area of substance. He seemed to care more about improving his style than improving his mind. We drifted apart after high school, checking in for meaningless conversations every few months. It was in between one of those months that I decided to text him something I had been thinking about. I had been working on the memoir for a couple hours, but kept getting distracted. I was supposed to be finishing a chapter on one of Mary's hospital stays, but my mind kept wandering to another place. I thought about other adopted kids, about how straightforward their lives seemed in comparison to mine. I thought of Isaac, who seemed to blend in so well with his surroundings. He never mentioned his adoption, and never seemed to need to. His life spoke for itself. He was just "Isaac," a man perfectly content with the way his life had turned out. However, one thing was needling me. If he was so content, why he had he felt the need to change his last name back to his birth name (Santana) 3 years ago? Why was Isaac Brenner no longer good enough? What made "Santana" necessary now? It was a thought I had pondered for years. Originally, I thought he was no longer close with his adoptive parents; that they had finally drifted to a point where he could no longer swim ashore.

I thought he had changed his name because "Santana" sounded flashier than Brenner. Isaac after all, was a flashy person, finding various ways to stand out from the crowd. He loved to describe himself, who he was, what he was doing, who he was with. That behavior did not change after he changed his name. He talked, he laughed, he rubbed elbows, he pounded his chest. I viewed the name to be yet another one of his masks, a simple stage name for him to build his image on. He refused to address his new name. It was something that just "was." It needed no introduction. However, part of me thought he might have had another reason to change his name. And so I texted him, asking what had prompted the change. He texted me back a minute later, giving me an answer that was expected but startling all the same. "Honestly, bro, that's just me," he said. "That's my birth name and it just felt right…ya know? Love my parents for the adoption but just want to carry on my bloodline. Ya feel me?"

"Yeah, I feel you man," I replied a minute later. "You're doing both families proud either way."

I was taken aback. I had no idea that he had cared about "carrying on the bloodline," as he called it. However, it was obvious that he felt a deep connection to his birth family, even though he had never gotten the chance to meet them. It was important to him that his future sons and daughters carried on the name of his mother and father. Still, the biggest talking point in his text message remained the quote "Honestly bro, that's just me." To a friend of Isaac's for over a decade, the line was like an onion. Never before had this been "just him," Isaac *Brenner* had been "just him." Now I was finding out he had been another person entirely—I got the impression that he felt the same way. "It's just who I really was," he had said.

"Who I was named by—my real parents—and that meant something to me." It was a little hard for me to stomach. Part of me felt as if Isaac's adoptive parents had failed him. Why else, at the age of 20, would he have felt the need to reclaim a part of him he felt he had lost? *Who I really was. My real parents.* The former sentence said that Isaac was never really Isaac Brenner. Although he loved his adoptive parents, he was never truly one with them. He was never their blood. His real parents were, and Isaac believed they had had a vision of him, a vision of the man they hoped he would become. Isaac Santana was that man, and Isaac felt it was time to recognize him.

The more I dissected it, the more Isaac's experience started to fall in line with that of the black girl, Janet. Both had been adopted by white parents, and both had felt the need to add to their identity so that it encompassed their entire cultural experience. Isaac's name change was less culturally motivated than the girl's revelation, but the message it sent was the same: *"I am separate from my adoptive family, and want to be recognized as such."* The fact that Isaac made a distinction between his adoptive parents and his "real parents" was telling, as well. Whether or not he made the distinction because he never felt culturally in tune with them or just failed to mesh with them was irrelevant. Either way left him an adopted child looking to redefine his true roots.

His story was one that gave my grandmother's worries credence. Isaac and others like him were living proof that even the best adoptive families were capable of failing their children when it came to matters of race and culture. His story was proof that the system had failed. Isaac, a successful businessman, had had to wait until he was an adult to discover and identify with his real family. Some would argue that even under these circumstances he had been lucky—that there were others who would never discover what it meant to identify with their "real" family.

It doesn't seem as if it would matter that other adopted children—Allison Rubin, David Zomosky—also children of transracial adoption, fully identified with their culture at early ages. It would not matter that in those cases, the parents made their kids research black and Korean history. It would not matter that Allison's father was a Civil Rights activist, a man who campaigned in Mississippi during Freedom Summer in 1964. It would not matter that David's parents made a point to cook Korean dishes, to take him to Korean events—but it should; because it is important.

As David put it "my adoptive parents didn't really stress anything on me. They actually worked to accept my heritage. They took me to Korean culture picnics, and introduced me to other Korean adoptees," he said. "If anything," he said, "I identify more with American culture, though."

David's responses in particular proved that when it came to culture in the transracial adoptive household, it was possible to have your cake and eat it, too. Because his parents exposed him to his cultural history at an early age, David was never in confusion about his own "cultural heritage" as he put it. However, because David's parents worked to make him an integral part of their family, of their block, neighborhood, and of their community, David was always reminded of his American heritage as well. He was raised in America, English was his first language, and he gravitated toward classic American pastimes—baseball, in particular. David is what America is becoming and has always been—multicultural. In cultural terms, David's story should serve as a model not only for adoptive kids, but for all kids as well. Any opportunity to learn about one's ancestors, whether from Rhode Island, or the Irish Isles, should be encouraged. David has not been able to locate his biological family, but has been conscious of his culture since the age of five, a testament to the power of education and acceptance.

Allison, a woman the same age as David, was also privy to both of these values. What is interesting is that even though she is conscious of her culture, she prefers to look at her current cultural identity in a different way than David. David's daily life consisted of items that outlined his past and present cultural heritage, vital pieces of his makeup with which he chose to define himself. Allison was more interested in being defined in name alone. When I brought up the point that there were those who felt that some who grew up in transracial adoptive households would grow to be racially confused individuals, Allison had this to say: "Yeah I disagree, I love myself and who I am. I find ignorance to be within people who think like that. I guess the ultimate barrier is getting past the race factor. I'm Allison whether I'm black, white, yellow, purple. That's who I am and that's all that matters. I guess individuals such as us are ahead of the times."

Allison's confession was that of a woman who recognized and defined herself in a manner separate from race. She understood the fact that she was black, but did feel as though that should be a focal point of who she was.

"My parents are very political and intellectuals, in a sense," she said. "They appreciate history. My dad was in SNCC and black history has always been ingrained in me. Because of that, it's never been something I felt I had to learn about, though," she said. "They actually stressed Judaism and politics, along with general morals, more than anything else. Black history was always important, never to the extent of it being a necessity given my family 'situation,' she said. "Ninety-nine-point-nine percent of the time I forget I'm adopted, people will bring it up from time to time, and I'm like—oh that's right, yes, yes that is correct," as I laughed heartily. "Shit is irrelevant for me," she added firmly.

I wanted to say that it was irrelevant for me, too—that I forgot I was adopted from time to time as well. However, I couldn't. I always remembered I was adopted— almost every day, in fact. It was impossible not to. Everywhere we went, people stared. Everywhere we went, people glanced at my family. Everywhere we went, people reminded us—reminded me. Allison felt differently. She recognized that her family was unique, but that was about it. Being an adopted child was not something that defined her identity. It was not something that made her "Allison."

She was adopted at the same age I was, but was able to escape the arduous custody battle. Her biological family was nowhere to be found, a harsh reality, but one in turn that created a different journey than she would have experienced had she known them. Her path to adulthood became more… straightforward, in many ways than my own. The fact that she often forgot she was adopted was not surprising. From the age of two, her family had raised her as their own, imparting the wisdom, morals, and religious beliefs their parents before them had passed down. Judaism was stressed more than black history, because both of Allison's parents formed much of their identity around their faith.

"If anything, people ask more about why I'm Jewish than why my parents are white," Allison said to me once. Her words spoke to her apathy about the race question, about the adoption question. To her, the only thing that mattered was that she was her parent's only daughter. When her parents died, she was the one who would carry on the family legacy. She wasn't just an adopted child—she was a Rubin. And as such, there were certain things that she embodied. Strength, sense of self, and moral character were all on the list. A perspective on history as well as a specific belief system was on the list as well. This is why she had had the foresight to recognize that there were specific struggles she would face as a black, Jewish, adopted woman raised as an only child. This is why she would continue to honor her faith, and pass it down to her children when the time presented itself. This is why she would talk openly and honestly with her children about sexuality. It was all part of a plan. A plan to be the best person she could be.

After speaking with Allison, I reflected on the adopted children I knew. All of them were raised by white people, and all of them were great people. All of them were genuinely nice people as well, individuals who would be described by their peers as caring and kind. I sat back and relaxed, typing letters in my mind. Who they became it seemed, regardless of their race, regardless of their gender, held a direct correlation with who raised them. If Isaac had not been surrounded by parents that fostered his love for soccer, he may not have identified with one of the only things still connecting him to his Columbian heritage. On the other hand, if Isaac had been surrounded by more culturally hands-on parents, he may have identified much sooner with his heritage than he did. He may have expressed interest in going to Columbia, in finding the town he was from. He may have been familiar with a Columbian dish or two. He may have shown more interest in actually learning Spanish. But he did not, and part of that was on Isaac himself.

He could have tried harder. He could have learned more. However, his parents could have played a bigger role as well. They could have gone the extra mile to make sure Isaac was in tune with both his Brenner and Santana sides. But maybe it was not in their character to do so. Maybe they were not in touch with their own culture, with their own family history. Maybe they weren't like Allison's parents, or David's. Maybe they did try to show Isaac a part of his culture at a young age. Maybe he simply wasn't into it. Maybe he needed to grow up a bit before he could appreciate what his parents had tried to teach him when he was younger.

I had no idea which armchair psychologist idea was correct, or if any of my ideas even made sense upon further review. The only thing I knew for certain was that children benefit from whom they are surrounded by. In this way Isaac, Allison, and David had been fortunate. Their parents had all been great.

However, I thought to myself. *What if they hadn't? What if the women and men that adopted my friends had been awful parents? What if they had gone off to party on Saturdays instead of taking their kids to a movie? What if they told them they would never amount to anything? Or, what if they had been fine parents, but had had no idea how to raise a child of a different race? What if they simply did not care if their children knew anything about their biological family? What if they lived in a community where their children never got to see anyone who looked like them?*

The questions were more important than the answers, and they were why my grandmother's lawyers were so interested in making sure the judge took them into consideration. I respect them for fighting. Any adopted child, black, white, or brown, is at risk of having bad parents. However, a child adopted by a family of a different race faces a more complicated set of issues. Indeed, the child adopted by the wrong family (whether that family is white, black, or brown), really *is* at risk of losing a part of their culture, or of never understanding it in the first place.

In Washington, D.C., then a mostly black city, this argument played fairly well to the judge. My grandmother's lawyer put it something like this: "We need all the strong, intelligent, and culturally aware African-American men we can get in a place where black men under 25 kill each other at an alarming rate. We need culturally aware black men to come back to the community and teach our youth how to stay on the right path. How can we do this, if we start throwing away our young men to white parents who may or may not care about the issues of the black youth?"

If I had had the social capacity for a rebuttal, I would have said this: "Black men are still overwhelmingly raised by black parents, and at this time the black population still struggles to prosper in relation to other races. Blacks have higher rates of incarceration, lower life expectancies, and lower education levels than any other racial group apart from Native Americans. Much of this can be attributed to socio-economic factors, but the fact remains that placing a black child in an all-black home far from guarantees that individual's success. A strong black home is great, however not every black home is great, and not every white home is bad. Each situation is an individual phenomenon. For the adoptive family, the mere act of choosing to adopt a black child in the first place shows an inclination toward open-mindedness that is conducive with a family who is ready and willing to foster the growth of the child who will not only be in tune with his or her own cultural history, but with his peer's cultural identity as well."

Alas, I was not a lawyer that day, and so my reflections as a twenty-something fell upon deaf ears. The lawyer was free to plow on with her message. Building upon momentum, Grandma's lawyer stood in court, boldly proclaiming "How will this boy, raised by *white, women*, become a healthy black *man*? How will he know *how* to be a man without a black, male influence by his side? What kind of an environment will he face when he goes to school? He will be ridiculed and teased by other children for the color of his parent's skin as well as the lifestyle they lead. It would be unfair and unjust to knowingly throw this child into a life of hardship in this way."

It was an argument that juries would eat up—if there had been a jury in this case, that is. As it was, there was only one judge, and thus one man who had the power to decide my fate and change the course of my life forever.

Chapter 14: Five Words

I always reminisce about the time I was in first grade. It was sometime in the spring, and my class was on an overnight field trip to Catoctin, Maryland. The trip was a Quaker retreat in which we were to learn more about nature and ourselves. S'mores, those tasty treats composed of marshmallows, graham crackers, and Hershey's chocolate bars, were also to be included. The trip was to be chaperoned, and so Mary volunteered her services. I was not particularly keen on having my mother join me on a class trip with my peers. However, Mary was cool on the trip, and everything worked out fine. The adults hung out with the adults, and the kids hung out with the kids. We spent our mornings relaxing by the pond and caught some fish along the way. In the afternoon we played Tarzan, swinging through the forest on a zip-line as our terrified parents looked on. As evening turned to night, the grownups cooked burgers and hot dogs, which we devoured with ease under a large gazebo.

I remember sitting with my friends and laughing about the day's events. Suddenly, I heard a shrill shriek, its sound familiar. I looked around before rushing out of the room, following the sound. I ran past several people before my path was impeded by a much bigger being. "Stay here, Tony," it uttered. Unfortunately, I had already made up my mind. I made a quick juke and ran to what seemed like a desolate patch of earth located just before the creek. Adults were huddled in a circle for reasons I could not ascertain. Then suddenly I knew why. In the middle of that circle stood Mary, looking as though someone had splashed water in her face. Tears flowed down her cheeks as shrieks of agony erupted from her body. Multiple parents were patting her shoulders and trying to console her, but their efforts seemed futile. She just kept shrieking the same five words: "They're going to take Tony! They're going to take Tony!"

she said, making herself madder every time she spoke; her voice cracking and her breathing heavy.

Many emotions coursed through my body. I was angry that someone had made my mother this angry, yet I also felt my mother's pain and agony as those words pierced my heart. It seemed as if Mary and I were the only two people who understood how much weight the words carried.

Above all, I was afraid. I had never seen Mary cry before, and now she was sobbing in front of 20 people. She had completely lost control of her emotions, a terrible omen.

We had become a family. And now, all of that seemed to be coming to an end.

I didn't tell my friends what had happened that day, and I didn't need to. They heard Mary's cries just as I had, and I'm sure they asked their parents what all the commotion was about.

My world remained one they could not understand. I felt as though I was literally going to be taken away at any moment by my grandmother, and was mentally prepared to say goodbye to my moms. I fully expected a car holding an older black woman would pull up to the campground and signal that it was time for me to go. Mary's shrieks had sounded *that* urgent.

The 3 $^{1/2}$-hour car ride back was one of the longest of my life. The car did not contain enough space to contain my expansive emotions, and by the time it rolled up to our driveway, I nearly flew out of the back seat. I pitter-pattered up our walkway and walked through the brown wooden door, afraid of what I might find.

Instantly I was greeted by the sight of Janet, who sat in a blue recliner in the corner. I tiptoed up to her, unable to discern whether or not she would have wanted me to announce my entrance.

"Sit," she said in trembling voice.

"What's going on?" I asked.

"They're trying to take you from us," she said in a determinedly measured voice.

So it was true then, Mary was right.

"The court has heard their appeal, and has decided to grant Ms. Davis custody of you," she said, her voice cracking.

"What does this mean?" I asked.

"It means everything will remain the same," Janet said, her voice more forceful than before.

"How?"

"We can still appeal this decision, and find another judge. Before we do that, though, I need to make sure you're on board. Tony, do you want to stay with us?"

"Yes," I said, my voice cracking a little bit now, too. "This is my home, and you're my parents, I would never want to be anywhere else."

It was at this point in time that Janet hugged me for what felt like hours. There were no words between us. Only the quiet sobs that echoed slightly, and the warm tears that hit the wooden floor lightly, gave the room any sign of life.

However, as the hours wore on and the evening turned to night, I realized that I was safe for at least another day.

Suddenly 1 day turned to 2; 2 days turned to 3. Before I knew it, a month had passed, and then a season. A year went by and I was still there. It turned out that during that time Janet and Mary were doing exactly what they said they would be—fighting. First they appealed the decision to the full District of Columbia Appeals Court. Their appeal was rejected, but two judges dissented, saying that the appeal should have been accepted on the grounds that same sex- parents were perfectly qualified to raise children. Next, they appealed to the United States Supreme Court. The Court declined to hear the case, but during the court proceedings, no legal action was allowed to be taken. The appeal to the Supreme Court was just a tactic. They never expected the court to take the case; they just wanted to buy time. They did. And nothing changed; I remained with Mary and Janet, while taking select Saturdays to spend with my grandmother. As the years passed both sides grew tired, or softened, and a compromise was finally reached.

I would live with Mary and Janet. They would raise me. My grandmother would get legal custody, while Mary and Janet would get legal as well as physical custody. The trial judge signed the agreement, and the deal was done.

For my grandmother, it was an overall win. She had been granted shared custody, which meant Mary and Janet were obligated to bring me over every other week, but she did not have physical custody, which meant she did not have to care for me on a daily basis like she had done so many other children in the family. She was off the hook. However she felt about my moms being gay could wait until I arrived at her house every other week. She would do no more fighting.

For my moms, it was the best outcome they could hope for. "I was going to stay right where I was, and nothing much was going to change," as Janet put it. For me, the outcome was a dream.

However on that night and other nights like it, I went to sleep only to be greeted by a nightmare. In it, a yellow cab came to pick me up as Janet and Mary looked on from a rain-soaked window. It was as if the life I spent with them was the actual dream, and that reality would soon be upon me.

Chapter 15: Cancer

I am very afraid. I don't want to die. I want to be a mother to my son, the son who I

worked so hard and so long not to lose. He is such a wonderful child and we are so

close. I want to be with Janet, my partner of 11 years. I want to love my friends and

work at my job and go mountain biking in the fall. I want to live.

That entry, dated 1997, was the year Mary started treatment for colon cancer. In 2001

she went into the hospital for good. The illness that had started in her colon had metastasized to

her liver. The doctors had to remove everything south of her small intestines, which meant that

she no longer had a colon. Mama described it this way in her journal.

I will no longer have an asshole. What a concept. Instead, I'll have a little (?) hole on

my side, a permanent colostomy. I tried explaining this procedure to Tony who

responded "Oh my God, Mommy, you'll have to lie sideways on the toilet to go to the

bathroom!" After I finished laughing, I explained about the colostomy bag. His

observation was "Well that will be weird but at least you won't have to go look for a

bathroom." I do appreciate his perspective.

Mary's colostomy bag was not the only change her body would have to undergo. Her

freckled yet tan Irish skin was now a tinge of pale yellow due to jaundice, a condition in which

the liver produces an excess amount of bile. Her yellow pigment came from the chemical

bilirubin, a byproduct of old red blood cells. In addition to this, Mary was also going through

intense chemotherapy, which is an attempt to eradicate the cancer by flushing mass amounts of other harmful toxins into the body. The subsequent treatments left her weak physically; she was no longer able to bike through Sligo Creek Park on Sunday, coach my soccer games on Saturday, and walk our rambunctious mutt Harriet on Friday.

I would like to tell you that Janet and I visited Mary in the hospital whenever we could, however this is not true; it felt more like we visited Mary in the hospital whenever it was appropriate. Our visits came not because we wanted to go, but because we knew it was the right thing to do. The actual act of visiting felt more like a chore than anything else. Indeed, visiting a sick loved one in the hospital was not my idea of fun.

After a long day of school, tons of third grade multiplication tables to do, and a stomach that pains for a hearty meal, all I want is pizza and sleep. My feet hurt from the double duty of playing soccer in PE class and then playing it again with friends in the afterschool program.

It's 5:30 and school ended 2 $^{1/2}$ hours ago. "Where is Janet?" I asked myself. "I thought she was coming at five." The counselors are busy flirting with each other and all my friends have gone home. Only a dozen children remain. One by one they get picked up, the smiles on their faces signaling their early release from prison. Unfortunately, my stay in this place isn't up quite yet. "Where is Janet?", I ask myself again.

"There!" There she is. All right now, I'm finally going home, finally.

"All right, champ, you ready to go to Holy Cross?" She says as I slide into the Blue Subaru.

"Yes," I answer solemnly, my hopes of freedom dashed yet again.

"Okay, then," she says brusquely as we head off into the sunset, both aware that the day is far from over.

We drive for what seems like an eternity. Holy Cross is only 6 miles away, but it takes us over a half-hour to get there with the traffic. We step out of the car slowly and stretch before walking through the sliding glass doors. Upon entering, we're greeted by the smiling nurse at the counter. I look around, taking the hospital in as I always do.

Holy Cross smells like stale bed linens…reeks of old people, and the walls are painted hospital blue. Hospital blue is the most boring blue there is, designed to be pale, lifeless, and uninspiring. The cafeteria smells no different from the rest of the hospital and the food is, to say the least, as uninspired as the hospital's walls. A creative night for the chefs would include the decision to put barbeque sauce instead of ketchup on the tater tots.

Mary's room is on the third floor. We take the steel gray elevator up before the doors open, showering us in a pale yellow light. We step out into the empty corridor. A middle-aged nurse wheeled an old man with an IV attached to his wrist who keeps his gaze downward toward the gray and white tiled floor as we pass. The hall is very silent, the only noises coming from the blare of the TVs in various rooms. Some people seem to be watching game shows; others watch old movies on HBO. Mary happens to be watching the news.

She greets us with a toothy grin and beckons us to sit down on two old dusty chairs by her bedside as we muddle in. Her black hair is less thick than it once was but is still a curly mess. Her face appears bloated and her skin is yellow. However, her spirits on this occasion appear high. She starts a conversation with Janet about the latest political happening as they talk back and forth about things I do not fully grasp. Bored, I plop down on the gray sofa adjacent to the bed and turn on my beloved cartoons. A few minutes later I'm prompted to take a brief glance away from my riveting show to look up at Mary as her supper arrives. The food she eats is not appetizing in the least. It is some kind of corn and some kind of meat, brought out to her on wheels by the nice, middle-aged nurse we saw earlier.

The food sits on a tray that looks as if it should have cat food on it. Mary looks at it with disdain. The JELL-O seems to be the only thing she is able to look at without wincing and I don't blame her. By the time she is finished picking at her food, evening has turned into night and it is almost time for Janet and me to leave. I turn off the TV and turn to my moms. Both seem happier than the occasion should warrant. Janet is smiling effervescently, and Mary seems to be having the time of her life as she makes an apparent joke I didn't catch in between *Rugrats* scenes.

They kiss each other goodbye as I look on, a sour expression on my face. Mary proceeds to kiss me on the cheek and mentions as she does every time to stay on the right path in school and get good grades. Janet and I leave and have some hospital food from the cafeteria on our way out. It is surprisingly okay; however my expectations have been lowered significantly due to the food Mary received and the protests uttered by my hunger-starved belly. I proceed to demolish it in a manner that would have impressed a professional Sumo wrestler. The moment after I finish the last bite, I feel my shoulders relax. My mind shifts to a more positive place. *Everything will be all right, I tell myself. Mary did not look good today, but she seemed much more energetic than she did upon my last visit. She's strong and she will beat this in no time. The three of us have endured a life fraught with drama, but it will all be over soon, and our family will be together once more...*

Chapter 16: Fielding Questions

In the meantime however, Janet and I are to cohabitate for the first time without Mary as a buffer for our colorful arguments. Our first few weeks alone together weren't exactly a walk in the park. Nothing physical takes place, but the neighbors certainly would have thought so due to the early-morning shouting matches.

The problem is that we are both very stubborn individuals. Neither of us ever wants to concede being wrong to the other person, and so when we argue, we cling harder and harder to our positions.

Janet's short temper was more evident, but I had one, too. Whenever I started to get mad, a sudden rush of emotion came over me, readying my anger to snap at any comment I felt was off the mark in some way.

Some mornings, I would feel the anger rising before Janet even stepped foot in my disheveled room. The sound of her footsteps stomping up the stairs alone were enough to annoy me before the lights were even turned on.

Its 6:56am. Why is she waking me up now? I have 4 more minutes to sit here, I would think to myself.

"I'm up." I would proclaim in the grumpiest voice I could muster as she entered the room. After rising out of bed, I would slowly follow her downstairs, spurred on by loud commands to come eat my yogurt.

I strolled into the kitchen and pulled the yogurt out of the fridge with great disdain. It was plain, it was boring, and it only wanted to be eaten by me. Janet made sure that it was never disappointed. Every morning it was eaten, and almost every morning I wished it wasn't.

Janet normally got upset over the time and care I put into dissecting it. The rate at which I "savored" it contributed to me being late for school, and her for work. Needless to say "Finish it!" was a common phrase uttered on Mondays, Tuesdays, Wednesdays, and well... you get the picture.

Sometimes, I moved with deliberate slowness in the morning just to piss her off. My need to prove some kind of point came to take precedence over common courtesy more often than not. There were times at which everything she did irritated me. From the way she addressed me, to her continuously rising voice, to her knack for telling me to do things I was literally already in the process of doing. For instance, there were many times in which I tried to think two steps ahead of her by turning off a kitchen light or locking a door before she had a chance to tell me to do so. This particular strategy worked for a while, but eventually I always ended up making a mistake, and Janet was always right there to point it out. Her green eyes were always lurking, watching my every move as I got up to turn off the light. If I hesitated for just a second, her mouth was sure to move.

"Turn off the light," she would say in a commanding tone.

My body would always tense up in a vain attempt to control the anger that was sure to come.

She got me. *Again. Dammit. Can't she see I'm already doing it?*

On a good day, I kept these thoughts to myself and simply turned off the light and went upstairs, annoyed, ready to put on some Eminem and zone out.

On a bad day however, I was sure to retort "I'm doing it!" with as much venom in my voice as possible. I would march upstairs and zone out to Alanis Morrissette once more, hoping the situation would resolve itself. However, tension between us would build, and before I knew it, her temper was shorter than it ever had been, and we would start shouting at one another with more gusto than ever before.

Janet's job in our shouting matches was to initiate the yelling. My job was to respond in kind with whatever immature response I could muster. I never feared physical retribution, and knew that Janet loved me too much to throw me out of the house. This knowledge allowed me to wisecrack without having to worry about a muzzle being affixed to my head. And since physical punishment was off the table, my only fear became the possible loss of privileges. I could only argue for so long before I began to lose TV, socializing, video games, and soccer playing rights.

My ultimate goal was to navigate those verbal wars without losing any of those privileges. The trick was managing to find out what privileges I was willing to lose as my anger rose.

One week, I may have been willing to lose socializing privileges because I didn't have plans that weekend. However, when I *did* have plans, I was willing to lose my TV privileges. I had it worked out to a science. The only snag was that I rarely tended to lose just *one* privilege. If I lost TV privileges, I had probably already lost socializing and video game privileges, as well. If I had lost video game privileges, I had probably already lost soccer privileges.

Indeed, whenever Janet's voice reached opera-singer levels, I knew I was damned to a weekend of heartache. Still, I always tried to talk my way out of it—and I always failed. The only way to have a chance at coming back from the brink of destruction was to speak to her when the storm had calmed, at which point it was safe to stick my head downstairs and check the temperature.

Phew. All right the coast is clear, I would tell myself. *Now I can make my case. Saunters down the stairs, turns to face Janet, who sits on blue couch five paces away.*

"Mom, I wanted to apologize for how I acted earlier." I began.

"I may get angry from time to time, but I still love you, and never set out to make you mad. I just get frustrated when you yell. Still, I shouldn't have responded the way I did. I know I was being immature. I have to grow up and just listen to what you say and move on. You are the adult, and I am the child. I respect that, and will not question you when you give me an order. I understand how much you do for me and for the family in general. I understand that you are the one who takes care of Mama's medical bills, works 60-hour weeks, and still finds time to take me to soccer games. I know it has to be stressful and I appreciate you always being there for me. I know that they don't offer you a lot of flexibility at work, and understand how that would make you less patient than you would normally be. You are basically raising me by yourself, and I know that can't be easy, especially when I make your life more difficult than it has to be."

This apology was given… about once a month. Janet and I both knew that we would eventually fight again, but it always felt nice to have some peace in the household for a spell while we took turns honoring each other. I knew that Janet would try her best to be patient with me, and she knew that I would do as she said without too much semblance of attitude. It was the best arrangement either of us could ask for.

Indeed, the fact that we were able to get along for any period of time at all was a vast improvement over years past. I recall many times in which Mary had to tell us to behave ourselves when she went off to save the world.

"And no shouting from you two, it drives me crazy," she would say.

"God, Mary, everything will be fine!" Janet would exclaim.

On most occasions, I still thought Mary was in my corner regardless of what had transpired. Whenever she took Janet's side, I felt that she was simply putting her spouse before her child.

After all, Janet and Mary had been together as long as I had been alive. I was a "new" if not invaluable piece in the family fabric, but I understood that the bond they had went far beyond me. It was for this reason they were bound to keep up a united front of sorts in the face of a cranky child.

However, according to the words in Mary's journal, my assessment was slightly off the mark. For example, an entry written on June 26, 1997 reads: *Janet and Tony came over at about 5:30 in high drama. Janet's first words were 'He's lucky to be alive right now!' Pointing at Tony. 'What happened?' I asked. 'Did he have an accident?' 'No!' She nearly shouted. 'He interrupted my telephone call with the insurance agency by picking up the upstairs line while I was on the downstairs line, while I was talking about the reimbursement for your first CAT scan. I **told** him to leave me alone when I was on the phone.' Tony, of course, simply whined, whimpered and cried during Janet's outburst then heaved a sob and cried, 'no one listens to me! I asked you to listen to me! Nobody cares.' 'Just eat your dinner,' said Janet, shoving the cut-up chicken in his direction.*

I was woozy from the pain meds but I had to deal with these sobbing, bug-eyed people who looked like they were ready to kill each other. I sent Janet out to get her own dinner and told her to get it from out of the hospital so she could relax. Tony collapsed in my arms, whimpering. He told me that he was hurt because the camp director and kids at camp didn't care that I was in the hospital and that his Mommy was not at home. Poor kid, he was genuinely hurt.

When Janet came back, she was in a better humor and decided to go buy Tony some new pajamas and underwear. In the meantime, I gave Tony a shower and read Goosebumps *to him. He began smiling and giggling and cuddling with me in the bed. He and Janet made their peace over a new pair of Chicago Bulls pajamas for Tony. By the time they left, he was hugging and kissing Janet. I'm glad that even in the hospital, I can soothe my family.*

6/18/97

This entry was written during Mary's first stint in the hospital. In it, she paints the picture of a woman simply trying to save her family from unnecessary stress during a trying time. She must have known that there would be a time in which Janet and I would have only each other to lean on. Even then I knew she was right, but I hardly expected the situation to present itself any time soon.

I remember picturing life without her, and it just didn't seem to fit. She was 33. She was going to live to see me marry. She was going to live to see me buy a home. She was going to live to see me father children of my own.

Up until that point, when I pictured a parent dying, it had been Janet lying in a coffin. After all, at the time they took me in, Janet was 47 and Mary was 28. The logical assumption was that Janet would live to see me hit 35 and pass away soon after.

I figured 35 was an all right age to deal with death, and for Janet, it allotted enough time to teach me all about life and see the historic milestones parents dream of for their kids. Everything would be a natural progression, an organic happening.

Unfortunately, untimely death can be a natural progression as well. Tumors, ugly though they may be, are also natural. The average person knows this, but rarely ever thinks this fate will befall them. When scenes of premature death *are* thought of, they are similar to how some Americans like their food: quick and easy.

The phrase "you could get hit by a bus tomorrow!" seems to be a fan favorite, when in reality getting hit by a bus remains substantially less likely to happen than contracting a fatal medical condition. Still, this has not stopped millions from uttering the phrase, anyway. Indeed, the very idea of getting struck by a bus seems utterly romantic. Waking up and going to work one minute, and dying the next, erase the trials and tribulations of life in one swift moment. Everyone dreams of it: the crash. The loved ones huddled by the bedside. The crowd that shows up for the funeral. The tears of the parents, the kind words of the crestfallen friends, the faraway look in a former lover's eyes... all make the occasion more profound than any birthday party could ever be. The birthday party is an occasion in which friends come together to celebrate *with* the individual. The funeral is an occasion in which friends come together to celebrate *the* individual. It is a Hollywood ending befitting a rock star taken before his or her time, which is exactly who many of us dream to be.

Unfortunately though, death does not take place on a movie set. The camera does not fade to black as the characters walk away from the casket, and the people do not move into the next season as if their loved ones never left them. Most people know this, which is why they remain firmly planted on the earth. The pain of picturing their loved ones' prolonged heartache is too much to bear, too much to live for. Cursed, they settle for the mere dream of dying.

For most people, it remains a dream until old age. For those diagnosed with a terminal illness though, this dream often melds with reality, creating a scenario that forces them to doubt their identity and self-worth at a time that would otherwise be their prime.

Mary, for instance, struggled with no longer being able to do many of the things her body was able to do with ease just weeks before her cancer. She described it this way in July 1997:

"It all seems so unreal to me. I have always been an athlete. I run, I swim, I bike, I hike, lift weights. I even play rugby on occasion. My idea of fun is biking through the mountains, pumping my pedals through the remote back woods of Western Maryland. I coach my son's soccer team, darting around with ten hyperactive second graders. Sure, the anemia has made me fatigued and my running has suffered. But Jesus Christ, 2 days before I found out about the cancer I went on a 21- mile bike ride down the C&O Canal. I barely broke a sweat."

Such is the story of the fallen athlete diminished by a condition they have no physical propensity to overpower. They try to control the condition mentally, willing it into submission. However, when they find that this method fails as well, depression ensues, as it did with Mary.

There were several nights in which she could be seen with her shoulders slumped and her head bowed in a forlorn manner, silently mulling her fate in the darkness. I would lie next to her and pretend to be asleep, only faintly aware of my intrusion into her most intimate thoughts. She would quickly look in my direction just to make sure I was sleeping. After her doubts were alleviated, she began to pray, whispering these words:

Dear God, I just want to thank you for blessing me with such a loving family and such a beautiful child. I love him more than anything. I am willing to die for him. I know that now…

All that I ask is that you let me live long enough to see him graduate from high school. We have a tremendous bond, and I want the chance to see him grow into the great man I know he will be. I want to play a part in that ascension. God, please let me live to see that…

My entire body clenched in fear. It was as if she was publicly admitting defeat to a condition I previously thought wasn't life threatening. For the first time, the reality of her dying truly set in. What made matters worse is that her death seemed like less of a question of *if,* and more of a question of *when.* I found myself hoping against hope that God would answer her prayers and let her stay with me just a little while longer.

Chapter 17: Grey Skies

Unfortunately, God seemed busy doing other things, and in his absence, Mary's condition became noticeably worse. Her energy level dropped, and her weight ballooned due to the medication she was receiving. She no longer played soccer with me after school, or flew kites with me on the weekends. Instead, her hospital bed became her eternal oasis, an everlasting resting place hand tailored for the ill of the heart, mind, body, and soul.

It was at this time that friends and family began to take notice of how sick Mary was. Prayers in church were announced each week and whole meals were often brought to our family. Neighbors took to shouting "We got your back, Mary!" and "I know you'll beat it!" whenever they saw her.

In school, teachers offered their condolences and offered to help in any way they could. Everyone seemed to understand how important it was for our family to have a collective shoulder to cry on during our difficult process.

Still, sometimes peoples' need to offer support can get in the way of their better judgment. We want so badly to express how much we care for other people that we lose sight of how our own actions can sometimes make them feel worse in their time of grief. Such was the case on a bleak Wednesday in 1997.

It was midday, and our entire school was gathered on the ground floor for worship. About 150 of us sat there in number, ready to begin our weekly reflection session. The meeting started out normally enough. The lights were turned off, everyone was seated, and then complete silence fell upon the room.

After a few minutes, a quiet voice spoke out from the darkness.

"I just want to thank everyone in this room and everyone here at FCS for making my time here so enjoyable. After I moved, I thought I would never regain a sense of home. With your help, I have…"

Her voice faded into the background, and silence fell upon the room once more. Five unobtrusive minutes passed before another voice echoed out from the darkness.

"I just wanted to say a prayer for my grandmother who passed last month," the quiet voice said. "She was the nicest lady I have ever known, and she taught me a lot about life. Above all, she taught me to live with no regrets, and to be kind to all. I try to remember that every day…"

I looked around. Some seemed particularly touched by the girl's words. Heads were shaking, lips were clenched.

Her words had touched a nerve with me as well. I stared back down at the hard gray carpet, willing myself into an intense calm. I had all but zoned out, when a loud, scratchy voice pierced through my armor of silence.

"I just wanted to say a prayer for Tony," the voice said. "His mother has cancer and is going through a very difficult time. Please keep her and his family in your thoughts."

I suddenly felt hot. All of the eyes in the room were on me but I had nowhere to run. I turned to match the voice to the face, and soon caught the eye of Sarah Howard, a fourth grade teacher and the mom of my friend Sam. She crooked her neck in my direction and matched my gaze with a sympathetic one of her own. I turned from her and glanced blankly at the wall, willing the meeting to be over. After 15 merciless minutes, my wish was granted. I took great care to avoid all incoming eye contact as people shuffled around me, slowly unfurling from my Native American sitting style position before making my way to the door.

As we filed out into the hall, people stopped to greet me. Some offered their homes to me while others merely shook my hand. Either way I felt trapped, enveloped by a rush of emotion that sapped all of my energy. I looked for Sarah, but couldn't find her. I wanted to thank her in one breath, and blast her in another. She had invaded my personal space, my oasis of thought, using a tidal wave of words to crash on my fragile emotional shores.

I struggled through the throng, bobbing and weaving in her general direction. I appeared to be closing in when she seemingly vanished into thin air. In her wake stood more onlookers, a blur of people keen on capturing my every expression.

I headed north and sought out my friend Adam, whose presence brought calm in the midst of my anxiousness.

"I'm really sorry to hear about Mary, man." He said in an even voice.

"Thanks," I said.

The words sounded different coming from a friend. Adam knew Mary well, and must have been hurt by the news himself. His words felt real, because his feelings truly were.

We marched up the blue stairs and slowly made our way to the red handicapped ramp in front of the courtyard. All eyes still seemed to be on me, and I still felt completely unprepared for the situation at hand. People with listless faces jumped out and shook my hand; the whole scene gray and shattered in movement, like the most depressing flip-book ever made.

Suddenly, a scrawny, blond boy came barreling out of the crowd. He appeared dead set upon getting out whatever he had to say and was already out of breath by the time he reached his destination.

He turned slowly in my direction, struggling to hold his posture.

"Hey, Toooony," he said in a nasally sarcastic voice. "Sorry your mom has cannnncer." He added, stretching out every syllable.

His words were drawn out as if he had an audience (which, in fact, he did). He stared at me blankly, lost in his own grandeur. Were he to step back into reality, he would have felt his body being pushed to the ground as an angry black boy stood on top of him.

Chapter 18: Scenarios of Grandeur

A blank stare accompanied the blond boy's wonderment at his current predicament. Meanwhile the black boy straddled his chest, shouting angry words of discontent the blond boy struggled to decipher.

"What's wrong?" The blond boy stated in an anxious voice. "I was just saying I was sorry your mom has cancer!"

The black boy seemed taken aback at his words, loosening his upraised fist.

Was it possible that this blond boy was telling the truth? He asked himself. *Was it possible that he was overreacting?*

He looked into the blond boy's eyes. There was fear there. Fear from a boy who clearly felt he had something to lose.

This blond boy poses no immediate threat to me, he reasoned. *Still, he has disrespected my mother. He has to be dealt with.*

A small crowd makes a circle around the unfolding scene. Dozens of pairs of eyes can be seen darting to and fro as if incensed, awaiting the mayhem sure to ensue. Within seconds, the wait is over. The black boy has steadied the upper half of his body as if preparing to strike a finishing blow. He tenses his forearms and clenches his fists, bringing them slowly up in the air. Then it happens.

Both hands swing down as if released from a pendulum, slowly making their way into the blond boy's chest. The crowd lurches forward. The black boy pauses before quickly grabbing the neck of the blond boy. He wraps his fists around his vocal chords and squeezes just once before releasing him. The blond boy's face flushes in relief, aware that he could have suffered a much harsher fate. However, for some reason the black boy is still perched atop his sternum, ready to strike. The blond boy attempts to move but is thwarted by encasing hands. He screams in pain as his neck is pinched for what must feel like an eternity. It stops just as quickly as it began. The black boy hops off of his chest, turns from the crowd and walks away. His breath is fast and his pace is slow. He moves through the grass, steps on the concrete, and walks back up the steps where it all began. He opens the chipped red door, walks the few feet to his 1:30 math class, and takes his seat, only vaguely aware of the punishment he will soon face.

Chapter 19: The Beige Suit

I, of course, was the black boy, and the punishment I would face would be severe. However, I was less worried about what the school would do to me, than how the two soon-to-be-angry women at home would treat me when I arrived. This type of situation was unprecedented in our household, and so I had no general barometer of how my moms would react. All of my life, they had focused on molding me into the best gentlemen I could be. My napkin always had to be in my lap, my mouth always had to be closed when eating, and if I didn't hold a door open for a woman, I was sure to catch hell. My hair was always kept short, and my clothes were always far from ostentatious.

It was on that bleak Wednesday that I realized these seeming acts of mentorship held racial undertones. I had always suspected it, but now knew it to be true. Suddenly all of the talk about the importance of always being polite struck a greater chord, the lectures on never walking alone taking on a completely different meaning. In the past I had thought that I was being shielded from the random evils of the world. I had assumed that walking with a buddy was simply meant to protect me from robbers and pedophiles, and that always remaining polite would allow me to talk my way out of situations that would otherwise result in violence. What I had failed to realize was that my politeness, my careful thinking, my attentiveness, were all meant to keep the world from realizing that I was a young black male. It was as if I was wearing a beige-colored suit that prevented people from seeing my true race until I took off each individual article of clothing. Yelling stripped me of my tie, and walking alone at night stripped me of my shirt. Mary and Janet felt it was their duty to make sure I kept the suit on at all times, lest I be thrown out into a racist world that wouldn't accept the man I was under the tailored attire.

It was for this reason that I feared their reaction so much on that day. I knew that by fighting I had torn my suit, and that mending it would take special attention to detail. Another part of that fear, though, came from the realization that Janet and Mary were right in their attempt to put the suit on my person. They understood the horrors endured by the young men who had refused to wear it, and were not keen on letting their son suffer the same fate.

When they adopted me, the racial landscape was much different than it is today. America in 1993 was not a great place to be for the black man. Thousands were dying from homicide, and many more were spending the majority of their adult lives in prison. Mary and Janet were both social activists, and knew the statistics well. If they were to adopt a black boy, they knew that to protect him was to enable him to transcend race in whatever way possible. To be truly accepted, he would need to own a face that was neither black nor white. It was for this reason that they advised him to wear the suit, and become the best gentlemen he could be.

For a long time, I failed to live up to their expectations, keenly aware of my racial surroundings. When placed in a room with all black people I became anxious, unsure of what to say. Every time I opened my mouth I felt people looking right through me, a white boy posing as a black male—the beige man who had never taken off his suit.

I tried to adopt the slang, the slight slur in the voice, but I never felt comfortable doing it. In the end I always reverted back to how Mary, Janet, and I spoke at home, using big words that few kids my age (black or white) understood. More than one person said I was "talking white," intimating that I was trying too hard to be something I was not. However, what they failed to realize, was that it was only when I was imitating *their* manner of speech that I felt I was truly acting out of character.

As it was, I felt slightly better when placed in a room with all white people. Their culture was familiar to me. Their meat was dry, or always had gravy on it. They served cranberry with their turkey instead of greens. They had furniture that didn't squeak.

On paper, I surmised that this was the environment for me. However, something was amiss. I didn't walk around the room with the confidence bestowed upon the man who knows his surroundings. Every room was broken up into small circles of people, who formed subdued conversations in tiny pods at each space of carpet. I looked to and fro attempting to find the pod that contained a face similar to mine. When none appeared, I scrambled to the nearest patch, hoping a small island would take me in with open arms.

To my delight, one always did. As I shimmied my way into the circle, person after person smiled at me, complimenting me on what a nice young man I was. It felt great, but I still felt like there was something missing. It was as if I was a man masquerading as a caricature of himself. Yes, I knew how to speak and move and act like everybody else in the room, but that still did not make me feel as though I was like *everyone else*. No matter how hard I tried, I was never completely able to blend in, to transcend. Soon, however, I would feel the need to more than ever.

END OF PART 1

PART 2

Chapter 20: 11-Year Old Experiences

I awake to the sound of muffled coughing, hasty footsteps landed on a soft bedroom carpet before echoing against a hard wooden floor. I hear a loud "thud" as two knees drop violently to the ground. There is an audible "clank" as the toilet seat is lifted up and placed against the porcelain. The next sound I hear is vomiting, the excruciating retching of a woman who was my superhero... she inhales... and then vomits... she inhales... and then vomits once more. The loud, cavernous, bellowing angst that can be felt with each gurgle and each subsequent "plopping" into the once serene water, sound less like the vomiting of a drunk college freshman, and more like the sound of someone dying—someone dying a slow, painful death. My eyes dart to my door, where a thin line of yellow light emanates from the closed space. Two feet tiptoe into the bathroom—muffled conversation ensues.

"I think I need to go to the hospital, Janet." "Okay, okay, let's go."

"Who will watch Tony?" Mary says hastily.

"I'll call Martha, she can watch him for the night. Let's go," says Janet.

But they do not leave, not until Martha shows up. On the phone, they are assured she does not mind watching me for the night. Not until Janet and Mary make sure to thank Martha for her efforts, and not until Martha assures them that Tony will be taken care of. Ten quiet minutes ensue before she arrives, her gravelly voice signaling her entrance. They bid each other goodbye, the door creaks and slams shut, and everything is silent... more silent than I can ever remember...

I would wait through the night, unable to ascertain whether or not my mom is still alive. Martha shuffles downstairs, rummaging through an old bookcase to pass the time. I stare up at the ceiling, my neon stars growing fainter as the violet glow signaling a new dawn engulfs the room. My eyes hurt, and are surely red in color now. I have to pee, but don't feel like getting up. The overhead fan is still, creating a shadow of a black X on a white background. My eyes can no longer fight the urge, and close indefinitely.

Hours later, a door slams shut, waking me from my slumber. I yawn and open the curtain. The sun shines bright, flooding the room in color. I groggily turn over onto my side before stretching out, carefully slipping two cold feet onto a cold floor. I stand up, slowly making my way towards the door before stepping into a narrow hallway. I turn into the bathroom, lightly stepping on the rough tiled floor before lifting up the porcelain. The sound of the toilet draining echoes as I wash my hands. I gaze into the mirror, rubbing my eyes, before turning to the black towel rack to dry my hands. I leave the bathroom as Janet's voice echoes up the hallway.

"Mmm hmm, yes, yes. I didn't leave till around 6:00 a.m." Janet utters.

"Yes, yes, thanks again," Janet says.

"No problem, Tony was fine—anytime," Martha replies.

The front door opens once more before swiftly closing. I make my way downstairs, careful not to slip on the last step.

"Are you all right?" Janet says, staring me up and down.

"Yeah I'm fine." I reply. "How's mama?"

"Well—she is okay. She was having a tough time keeping anything down and was throwing up, but she has been given some fluids by the doctors. We can visit her later." Janet says.

"Okay," I said, knowing the situation was a little more serious than Janet was letting on. Indeed, when I had ventured into the bathroom earlier, I encountered several fresh red stains on the checkered floor. Mama was puking blood again. But, I couldn't let Janet know how much I knew. Her day had been hell already and I didn't want to make it any worse. I knew that in spite of my will to be treated like a grown-up, Janet still needed to feel like she could protect me from certain evils of the world. I wanted to scream to the heavens that I knew how sick Mama was, but felt it would benefit both of us to keep quiet. Having a typical parent-child dynamic was one of the only stable things we had left, and I didn't want to jeopardize it. Also, knowing that there were certain things Janet was neglecting to mention about each chemotherapy treatment gave me a sense of comfort. I did not want to know that Mary's liver was in danger of failing, or that several other dark masses had been spotted on other parts of her body, facts I learned years later. I just wanted to believe that she would still be alive in 10 years. And though I longed to be treated like an adult at age 11, I wasn't yet ready to be one.

However, on that day, I realized that soon, I would need to be. Mama had been sick before, but that cold December day was different. She wasn't just sick, she was ill.

I had a flashback to a day a few months prior. Janet and I had gone to Holy Cross to visit Mary on an icy evening. On our way to the entrance, Janet slipped and fell on black ice. When she stood up, her right eye was darker than the blue coat she was wearing.

"Are you okay?!" I had asked.

"Yeah, I'm fine," she uttered calmly, "I just need to put some ice on this."

"Okay. Here, let me help you," I said, gripping her left hand and putting an arm around her shoulder as we made our way up the path. "Thanks," she said. "It will be fine."

We meandered into the waiting room, taking the elevator up to mama's floor. As we stepped out, several people stared at us. We must have been more of an odd couple than usual, Janet's bruised face a beacon for all incoming passerby.

Mary was no less taken.

"Oh, my fucking God!" She exclaimed as we walked in.

"What happened?"

"I fell on some ice," Janet sighed. "I'll be all right; I'm going to get some ice for it." She said.

"Okay," Mary replied, "Tony and I will be here when you get back."

With a short wave, Janet left, leaving Mary and I alone.

Mary turned to me, a hurried manner about her. "Mom is not young anymore," she said quietly. "She is 56. Her bones are not as strong as they used to be. When she falls, she is more likely to break a bone," she said.

"If I'm not here," she said, "You need to be the man of the house," she said forcefully. "You need to take care of her."

I looked at her, unsure of what to say. She had never admitted that there might be a day in which she would no longer be around. She was the one who liked to embody strength, to stubbornly push on at all costs. She was the one who was adamant about beating cancer, about overcoming the greatest obstacle life had ever given her. She was adamant about it all, until now.

Her assertion that I needed to be the man of the house when she was gone was odd. It was as if she believed that she and I alone could function in this capacity; that Janet, by default, fulfilled the maternal role only.

It was odd, because it was Janet who taught me how to tie my first necktie; Janet who made sure all my buttons were in alignment. It was Janet who taught me how to use computers, how to fix the toilet, and how to put my new Legos together. Mary for her part did many of the activities expected of a classic matriarchal figure. She cleaned, she cooked, she arranged, she wore pearl earrings, all in the same day.

So what was she talking about? How was *she, alone*—the man of the house? Still, I understood her thought process. She did fulfill some patriarchal roles, and in our same-sex-parent household, gender roles still had their part to play. Voices like my grandmother's had claimed for years that the ideal home for a child boasted both a mother and father. Mary may have felt that by fulfilling both a patriarchal and matriarchal role within the household, she could prove them wrong. She did. On weekdays she worked into the night. On weekends she attended soccer games. She played good old dad and talked to me about women as well, even if the advice she gave was often what you would expect from a mom. "*Don't break too many hearts,*" she said. "*Save a dance for the fat girl,*" she said. However, it was still she that I looked up to, she I chose to emulate. It was her Alanis Morissette cassette tapes that littered the floor of my untidy room, her 35-pound dumbbells that I attempted to lift in the basement. It was she whom I acted like, strutting out my chest when playing checkers, too competitive for my own good. It was she who I knew would physically attack any careless burglars who dared enter our home. She was the rock, the woman who yelled the least, yet inspired the most fear when angry.

In her relationship with Janet as well, Mary may have felt as though she fulfilled the male gender role at times. Both she and Janet had good careers when they met, but Mary was the primary breadwinner, working at a prestigious law firm in Washington, D.C. Mary was also the original driving force in the decision to have kids. She decided she wanted to adopt, and although Janet agreed with her, it was Mary who brought the plan to light.

When I became a part of the family, it was Mary who volunteered to chaperone my class field trips. It was she who took me camping every few months, burning S'mores and filling canteens.

Still, Mary failed to realize that a similar case could be made for Janet as the patriarchal figure. When I screamed out at night, it was Janet who thumped into my room, scouring for monsters before tucking me in to tell me everything would be all right. When I needed help editing my papers and doing my math homework, it was Janet who took up the post. When there was yelling to be done and punishment to be doled out, it was Janet who stepped up to the plate. When Mary took me camping, it was Janet who collected the tent, the tarp, and the bike rack to fit over the car. It was she who bought the S'mores and instructed Mary on how to get to the camp site.

She was the godfather, the person behind the scenes who made everything run on time. However, so was Mary, just in different ways—I had two bosses in my life, two fathers, and two mothers. Two people striving to make me the best man I could be.

Janet walked back into hospital room as I awoke from my reverie, sporting a blue ice pack over her maroon-colored cheek. "Here, take a seat, mom." I said to Janet, getting up from my chair. "Thanks," she said, sitting down. Mary looked at me knowingly, as if I was beginning to fulfill my destiny. What she failed to comprehend in that moment, was that I was already the man of the house. She and Janet had taught me to be. And so I would always give up my seat to Janet, just as I would give up my seat to her. I had been raised to be strong, to find a way to make things work. Nothing—not even a death of a parent, would ever change that.

Some Facts

States and regions that explicitly allow for adoption by same-sex couples include California, Connecticut, Washington, D.C., Illinois, Indiana, Maine, Massachusetts, New Jersey, New York, Oregon and Vermont.

In states allowing gay individuals to adopt, Colorado, Ohio, Nebraska, and Wisconsin have laws preventing second-parent adoptions, meaning that only one parent is legally allowed to adopt. In these instances, the non-adoptive parent can at best be a legal guardian and is not subject to the hundreds of parental rights afforded to the full adoptive parent, including hospital visitation rights. In most states, whether gay adoption is legal is made on a case-by-case basis by a judge. However, there are 16 states that definitely allow joint gay adoptions (when a same-sex couple jointly petition for adoption): Arkansas, California, Colorado, Connecticut, Washington, D.C., Illinois, Indiana, Iowa, Maine, Massachusetts, Nevada, New Hampshire, New Jersey, New York, Oregon, Vermont, and Washington.

Still, people have successfully done second-parent adoption, meaning that while joint adoption is off the table, two individual parents can legally adopt a child separately. The following 16 states allow for second parent adoption: Alabama, Alaska, Delaware, Hawaii, Iowa, Louisiana, Maryland, Minnesota, Nevada, New Hampshire, New Mexico, North Carolina, Oregon, Rhode Island, Texas, and Washington.

Chapter 21: Parents

When people say that two women don't know how to raise a man, they are misinformed. In my household, as well as many other same-sex households in the nation, same-sex parents work overtime to make sure their children understand what it means to be a man or a woman in this world. Same-sex parents and their children are keenly aware that there are those who believe that their families are not equipped to raise a masculine man or a feminine woman. They are well aware that opponents of same-sex adoption argue that growing up in a same-sex household introduces children to a lifestyle in which gender roles are not clearly defined, causing possible confusion later in life. They are also well aware that the opposition will argue that this confusion will lead the child to be more open about sexual preferences, increasing the likelihood of same-sex relationships. As Richard Kohm, was quoted as stating: "The most loving man cannot teach a girl how to be a woman. The most loving woman cannot teach a boy how to be a man."

He means, for example, that the girl with two dads may feel ill at ease asking questions about her body to her two dads. She may feel as though her life is one in which she is constantly seeking out a female role model to identify with in the absence of one in the home. Her dads may have a lot of female friends for her to discuss her issues with, but some would argue that this should not be a substitute for the natural role a birth mother would play in her life. By contrast, the male with two moms may feel ill at ease discussing physical changes during puberty with his two moms.

I never had trouble discussing the latter, because I never felt it needed discussing. I had taken basic health class, and knew what was happening to my body. There were no discussions that needed to be had there. However, there were times in which I wished I had a father. Not a father *figure*, but a father. I wanted to imitate how he stood when he walked into a room. I wanted to ask him for advice about how to approach the girl I liked. I wanted him to sit and tell me what it meant to be a man.

In his absence though, I developed my own manly habits. I stopped crying when I fell down. I made sure my voice sounded deep. I excelled in sports. I looked at the people on my wall, all athletes. I gazed at their expressions, watching the intensity in their eyes as they rose up for an incredible dunk or a sensational catch. I turned to my peers, watching how they interacted with women, taking notes on the things I liked.

I was determined to be the best person—the best male I could be, regardless of my circumstance. I was constantly out to prove myself. I was never in confusion about what gender I was, or about what roles I was expected to fulfill. I knew that I was not alone in that regard— that other kids from same-sex households had to feel the way I felt. I simply did not have the evidence to prove it, and so I went hunting for an article. Within minutes I found one.

Golombok, Spencer, and Rutter had conducted a study on same-sex households. In their descriptive study, they found no evidence of gender identity confusion for any of the children evaluated in their study on same-sex-headed households; none of the children wished to be the other sex or consistently engaged in cross-gender behavior. No difference was found between children in lesbian and heterosexual families for either boys or girls, in regard to acting out behavior that was typical of their sex either. "Daughters of lesbian mothers were no less feminine, and the sons no less masculine, than the daughters and sons of heterosexual mothers."

Their findings are in direct contrast to the perceived fear of the "gender bending" that will occur within the lesbian- or gay-headed household. Indeed, "gender bending," and or "gender confusion" is deemed unlikely to occur, given the fact that children actively seek out gender-related information for themselves, and adopt behaviors that they perceive to be appropriate for their sex. Their findings showed that the actual source of gender roles came from gender stereotypes, and not only the parents. This explains how boys raised by single mothers are able to grow up to be well-adjusted men, and why girls raised by single fathers are able to grow up to be well-adjusted women.

***

What is difficult for some people to understand is that these studies—which highlight the strengths of the same-sex household—are just the tip of the iceberg. In future years, they will do more studies about us, the children of same-sex couples. They will begin to understand that many of us have been forced to look deep within ourselves to justify our masculinity or femininity to the outside world. It can happen to women and men, minorities and non-minorities, and both the well-adjusted and socially awkward.

I, for instance, feared being gay growing up. I was constantly looking for signs to improve my masculinity, to ensure my straightness. To me straightness was masculinity, masculinity was straightness. The coolest men in the world could go wherever they pleased and talk with whatever woman they wished to. They were idolized by boys and envied by men. They were athletic, strong, and unflappable. Attempting to embody anything less than what they possessed was not masculine. To be gay, was to be someone who could never truly be a "man's man", the antithesis of the straight man. To be gay meant embodying feminine qualities; softness, expressing one's emotions, spending too much time on one's physical appearance. It meant having platonic BFF relationships with women, and it meant wanting to form romantic ties with men. It meant that straight men would look at you funny if you were too nice to them for fear of being labeled gay themselves. It meant that it was harder to form a brotherhood with a fellow man, a pastime that the ideal male had mastered. It was not a race thing. This train of thought was common among Black, Asian, White, and Latino men whom I saw on the street, who I watched on television, and who I interacted with at school.

Being gay did not mean that you could not form close bonds with male peers. It did not mean that you would not be respected. However, it did mean that in some conversations you would feel left out, and that others might feel the need to leave you out. So much of what guys talk about (especially during adolescence) revolves around girls. Describing which girl you like, what you like about her, how to approach her when you ask her out for a date, what you did (or will do) on the date—are all important topics. Not being able to discuss these topics are almost like having no interest in sports. It is unnecessary to be good at sports. It is unnecessary to know anything about sports actually.

However, when the biggest sporting events happen, people flock to their TVs just to learn the basic facts so they have something minuscule to talk about at the water cooler. This applies to both men and women in this case. The situation is different when men discuss women. The man who has never dated can imagine his favorite girl. The "band geek" can discuss the girl in his class who also likes Marvel Comics. However, the gay man, the one who is comfortably out of the closet, cannot discuss the woman he likes with his fellow man after his friend talks about the girl he likes. He cannot talk about where he will take her, or what he will do. Someday soon, I hope that every gay man can talk openly about the man he likes at school with his heterosexual friend, and what he likes about the man. However, that time has not yet arrived. As such, there remains an element of popular "male" conversation that an openly gay male will have trouble discussing in a large group of male friends. He may not be ostracized, but the fact that he cannot discuss such a "significant" topic precludes him from being the alpha member of the group. This is because the alpha, as the most diverse male, is adept at talking about all subjects thrown his way from a relatable standpoint. The problem for the gay man comfortable in his own shoes in this hyper masculine structure is that there is one subject he is not able to relate to as freely as his fellow men are.

For these reasons I wanted to be straight, I needed to be straight. Not just for myself, but for my moms as well. I had to prove that all those people secretly ostracizing our family were wrong. I had to prove that I was a normal man in every way possible. No, it was more than that. I had to prove to people that I was the best man a man could possibly be. I had to prove that my two moms had raised the prototypical man's man, in every way. I had to show people like my grandmother how great our family really was.

I needed to be straight for myself as well. My moms had shown me photos of Matthew Sheppard in 1997, a gay man strung up on a fence and left to die by people who thought families like ours should not exist. I heard my fellow men ostracized, called "faggots" for walking a certain way, for talking a certain way. I saw my peers imitate "gay men," poking their jaws out, using inflections in their voices. I saw Ryan Secrest and Simon Cowell poke fun at one another on national television by inferring the other was gay. I heard my relatives talk about "the faggots over there in Georgetown catching AIDS." I heard it all, and didn't want to see any of it. I couldn't be shut out from society. I couldn't take facing the world like that, a man constantly on edge about how others regarded his sexuality.

I couldn't take being denied my manhood. I had seen how society took even that away from the gay male. How they emasculated him, putting him in makeup and dresses in their movies. I had seen how they treated him in their military, denying him the right to speak about whom he loved, until "Don't Ask, Don't Tell" was finally and rightfully overturned. I had seen how they spoke of him even when they accepted him; speaking of him like an ugly insatiable ex-girlfriend who was cool with them as long as he didn't start flirting. I had heard their jokes, but more importantly I had seen their fear. They, straight men, were just as afraid of being gay as I was. It was for this reason that they constantly affirmed their manhood, using the phrase "no homo" and overdoing their gay male impersonations, decrying any statement or action that would draw suspicion of their sexuality. The only difference between them and me was that I was raised by gay people. I was already associated with it, more open to it, more suspicious.

I had to hide it, had to distance myself from it. No one could know whom I was raised by if I could avoid it. And I could avoid it. I could say "parents" instead of moms. I could say "my mom feels," instead of "my moms feel." I could cover myself. Most importantly, I could look deep within myself to ensure I wasn't gay. I could build that last layer of invincibility against any suspicion others might have. I could test myself, examining whether or not I felt sexually attracted to the men on TV. I could make sure.

Some days became harder than others, though. Sometimes I really did think I might be attracted to males. I would have a spilt second recognition that a male was attractive, leading me to question myself. I would question why I hadn't kissed a girl yet, leading me to question myself again. I became so worried that one day when I was 14, I resolved that if I turned out to be gay, I was never going to tell anyone.

I had heard of the people talking behind my moms' backs when they had adopted me, saying that lesbian women shouldn't adopt. I surmised that they didn't need to worry about their son facing the same type of discrimination. My grandmother certainly didn't need to know either, her distaste for homosexuality was well known, and didn't need to be reinforced.

Indeed, the best thing for me to do was to remain silent and live the rest of my life in misery. I was fully prepared to do so. I was a soldier, ready to sacrifice it all for my family. If I had to live the rest of my life in the closet it was okay, because my family would be rewarded. People would see our greatness, politicians would see our greatness. My grandmother would see our greatness. It would all be worth it, I just had to hold on for another—60 years or so.

Yes I was prepared to do that, at least, until I remembered how much I loved women. At least until I remembered that at almost every point in my life, I had had a crush on at least one girl in my class, neighborhood, or Sunday school. I reminisced about my pre-school crush Ariana, who was "stolen" from me by my friend Josh. I thought about Sara Huffman, who I imagined kissing in Sunday school class. I thought about my previous babysitter, who had 5 years and 6 inches on me. I thought about Rikki, the apple of my eye since kindergarten. I thought about the way I felt about all of them, the flutter in my heart when each of them entered the room, the stutter in my voice when I attempted to say something clever. I certainly didn't stutter too much around any of my guy friends, and my heart definitely didn't flutter when any of them entered the room. I guess I wasn't as gay as I thought I was, which was a relief, mainly because I knew I was not a good soldier. I valued happiness over everything, and knew that if I was gay, that fact would not cease to be true. In order to be happy, I would need to be *out,* which would require an entirely new level of bravery. A bravery which I just did not envision having.

However, I have to thank this process. It made me a more sexually aware individual, and more comfortable in my own skin. I had already done all of the internal tests, the questioning, the introspection, and I had come out all right. The words of a homophobe or a friend could not hurt me. When I went over to my grandmother's, I was prepared.

When an aunt asked me a question about my love life and my grandmother interrupted and said "You know that boy don't like girls." I was prepared. When she stated, "I know people over there and I know who you been going out with." I was prepared. Her words, harsh as they may have been, simply represented more internal tests— tests I continued to pass with flying colors.

"Nope, I like women," I said once. "Yes Grandma, I do have a boyfriend." I said sardonically another time as she smirked along. I continued to laugh, still unsure of whether she believed what she was saying. She liked to make fun of everybody, but her jokes often had grains of truth in them. When she professed that she had "spies" in my area, it sounded ridiculous, but her tone *had* remained strong. However, what I learned after all those years of soul searching, was that her words were irrelevant. I alone gave them power. If I felt her claims were ridiculous, then they were. If she asked me who I liked, I either told her or joked with her. I was defensive in neither case.

I kept telling myself that if I could handle her, I could handle anyone. If I wanted to make an impact on affecting policy in the battle for gay rights, I would have to. I would have to tell my story as well, which would mean opening myself up to people just as misinformed as my grandmother was. In order to tell it correctly, I would have to examine my life in a more honest way than I ever had before. People were not looking for politically correct answers, they were looking for the truth. To find it, I would have to find the strength so many within the same-sex headed household had already mastered.

Chapter 22: Speech Lessons

Contrary to what some believe, same-sex couples do not go into adoption with their eyes closed, they understand how some will look at their family, their sons, their daughters. As one gay parent, surmised: "As gay and lesbian parents, we are all under the stress of knowing that some people harbor violently negative feelings about our families. It is an awareness that may remain a mere whisper in the dim recesses of our consciousness or move to the foreground with frightening clarity, but it is an ongoing part of our lives. Each time we address the issue of our visibility, we balance our ideals, our politics, our hopes for support, and our parenting goals against our caution, our need for privacy, and our fatigue."

The same can be said for children of gay and lesbian parents, who understand the risks associated with growing up in a family structure thought to be sinful to many. They understand the risks, which is why they work so hard to be open individuals, to be accepting of others, and to respect the cultural traditions of other families. They know what it feels like to feel excluded, which is why they make sure others never have to feel uncomfortable around them.

For me, this sentiment manifested itself in how I chose to interact with my Christian peers. Some of them wore their faith on their sleeves, others did not. Some prayed before every meal, others did not. However in both cases one thing was clear—they felt attacked. They said the media kept saying they were evil, that they spread hate. That they attacked every gay person they saw. They felt as though they were being portrayed as homophobes who wanted all gays burned at the stake. They felt as though their country was being taken over by a liberal media who wanted to shove abortion and same-sex couples down their throats as if the Bible hadn't condemned both. They felt as if they were the minority, and that soon the country would try to eradicate their way of thinking through new laws and initiatives. In regard to the latter, they had

a point. Several states in the nation allowed civil unions for same sex couples, and several

others had made gay marriage legal.

Most Christians were fine with gay people individually, but the Bible said it wasn't right

for them to be with each other (romantically), and although they loved their gay friend,

neighbor, or cousin, they just couldn't bring themselves to endorse a union they felt violated

God's law. If I was in their shoes, I cannot say I would have felt any differently; if I was raised

my entire life with the knowledge that homosexuality was wrong—even evil—it would be hard

to go out and vote for same-sex marriage. It might be harder still, to form a friendship with the

child of a same-sex couple, knowing full well that I didn't approve of the "lifestyle" lead by his

or her parents.

People tend to form close ties with people whose familial background is similar to

theirs. It's why children of single-parent homes often marry other children of single-parent

homes, and why children from two-parent heterosexual households marry other children from a

similar household.

I worried that my familial background would be too different from my friends for us to

be able to connect fully. However, as I grew older, I learned that my friends were more open

than I thought, and wouldn't let something as simple as who I was raised by stand in the way of

our friendship. On the contrary, most people I told my story to expressed the same curiosity that

the blond boy at FCS had. They liked the fact that I was unique, and didn't see me any

differently after they found out I was raised by two wonderful women. Still, this is not to say

that everyone to whom I told my story was on board with the idea of the boy with two moms.

***

One example took place in college. It was the second semester of my freshman year, and my friends and I were sitting at a beige circular table in the school's dining hall. Everyone's plates were now empty, occupied only by mushy mashed potato crumbs and bloody meat stains. We laughed as we took turns doing impressions of one another, our voices getting higher as our hands gesticulated enthusiastically. I looked around at Jessie and Chris, who were deeply embroiled in a conversation on homosexuality.

"So, what would you do if your son was gay?" Jessie said.

"That depends," Chris said.

"Would you make him move out of the house?" Jessie said aggressively.

"Well, again, that depends," Chris said. "I mean I would love him no matter what, but if he had brothers I couldn't let them be exposed to that. He would have to live somewhere else."

"So would you disown him?" Jessie said.

"No," Chris said. "I would never disown my son, but if he's gay, I wouldn't want his brothers exposed to that lifestyle because it might rub off on them, too. If he wants to live that way it's his life, but I can't let his brothers grow up thinking it's okay when it's not. God says its wrong, and it is."

"So, do you think your kids would be gay if they grew up with him?" Jessie said.

"I don't necessarily think they would be gay..." Chris said, trailing off. "I just think they would be more open to being it. Like—kids emulate what their siblings do. If they saw that their brother was gay they might think, "Hey, maybe I should try it out, too," Chris said in a matter of fact tone. "I mean that's why I think gays shouldn't really raise kids, either," he added.

Our friend Rose spoke up for the first time, her voice bursting from two seats over. "But Tony was raised by gay people!" she said cheerfully, turning to me. Chris paused, clearly at a loss for words. Silence surrounded the table as Rose looked at me expectantly. "Yeah," I said quietly. "I was raised by two women."

"Shut up, no you weren't," Chris said playfully, cracking a grin.

"No, it's true," I said flatly, "I was." Jessie nodded in approval. "Yeah, it's true, man," he said seriously. "I know, I didn't believe it either the first time he told me," he added, laughing. "Oh." Chris said. "I didn't know, man. I mean, when I saw your mom I honestly just thought you had a white mom and that your dad was dark or something," he said, chuckling.

"No, man," I said, smirking. "I was adopted by two white women when I was five."

"Oh, wow," Chris said before recovering. "Okay—but you were raised by two *women* though. If you were raised by two men, then it would be different. You were raised by lesbians, so you were more inclined to like women. Kids who are raised by same-sex parents who are the same gender as their parents are probably gay in a lot of cases."

"Umm," I said reluctantly. "That's not true. There have been numerous sociological studies done on children of same-sex households, and all of the research so far has found that children of same-sex parents are just as well adjusted, and just as straight, as kids from heterosexual-headed households, regardless of what gender their parents are. "Also," I said. "I just really feel that being gay is not a choice. I can say from personal experience that growing up with gay parents might actually make you *less* likely to be gay because of what you witness your parents going through. I just feel like—who would choose that? You know? Who would *choose* to be on the margins of society in that way?" I added. Chris's face read like that of someone who wanted to listen, so I continued. "And I'm not talking about college girls who decide to experiment," I said forcefully. "For them, yes, it's a choice. However, same-sex parents who choose to adopt have known that they were gay from a very young age, and I believe that they were just born that way. I remember asking my mom about it and she said, 'You know—I dated a man in high school, but it never really felt right. I think I always knew, I just dated because that's what people were expected to do. But as I grew older, I realized that it was more important for me to be happy.' "

"Now—my mom grew up in the 50s and 60s," I said. "Being gay wasn't even something that was talked about. Yet she knew that she liked women even then. She grew up in a heterosexual household, and her sister is straight. Her family background had nothing to do with her sexuality, she just knew she was gay." I said. "The same thing can be said for every gay person I encountered growing up. They never 'switched sides,' or decided to live this different lifestyle. It was just who they were, ya know?" I added.

Chris looked at me as though seeing me for the first time. "Wow, I never knew that." He said shortly.

"Yeah, I mean it's my life," I added obviously. "It's how I was raised. The good you see in me from time to time is all them." I added sarcastically, an arrogant grin on my face.

I looked to Chris for a sign of life, but he just sat there, unmoved. It was if he'd been hit by a stupid pill that rendered him useless.

"I think it's cool," Rose said out of the blue, smiling. "Unique."

"Yeah, I agree," Jessie said. "Honestly if you hadn't told me I would never have guessed, man," he added as flashbacks of fifth grade entered my thoughts.

"Well, everybody ready?" Rose said. "Yeah, I'm ready," I said, still looking at Chris. "Yeah, let's dip," Jessie said, scooping up his jacket." Chris moved too—slowly, avoiding my gaze as he picked up his jacket. We walked out, passing several attractive co-eds on our way. I said goodbye to one as we walked back to our dorm hall, a touch of awkwardness in the air.

Chris was as animated and jovial as usual—just not with me. His baritone, cavernous laugh could be heard as we retreated to our rooms, each bidding each other goodbye.

Hours later my friend Bernadette was in my room, talking about what she had witnessed at lunch. "So that was awkward," she said. "Yeah," I said timidly, chuckling. "It was a little awkward." I didn't expect that topic to come up at all," she said flatly. "Yeah, I don't even remember how it came up," I said.

"So how do you think Chris took it?" She said inquisitively. "I don't know," I said slowly. "It was kind of hard to read him. I think that he definitely listened though, it felt like I was giving him a new perspective to look at."

"I think he learned something," Bernadette chimed in merrily.

"I do, too," I said, smiling at her. "I know that he's pretty um—devout, in his faith," I added shortly. "I know I won't change his mind about certain things, but hopefully he realizes that gay people are just normal people now. Hopefully he realizes that they don't go around parading their sexuality."

"I think he does—or will," Bernadette said. "I don't think Chris has really interacted with gay people before. When you were speaking it looked like he was contemplating a lot," she said.

"Yeah, it did," I cut across. "That's all I can really ask for… still, disowning someone is a pretty bad thing to do, no matter what the case… I hope he reconsiders his stance on that." I said, sighing. "I mean, I know he said that he would still love his son but if you're kicking him out of the house, you are basically disowning him. It's just hard for me to see that being the right thing to do as a Christian," I said, a disappointed look on my face.

"I agree," Bernadette said, scooting closer to me. "Chris has this diluted sense of what it means to be a man. He is very 'macho.' I think he was surprised when Jessie asserted that he could have a son that was gay," she said wearily.

I nodded, "I think he thinks he's too much of a man to ever be able to produce a son that would be a 'sissy.' " I said. "But Chris is a good guy overall, it's not his fault. It's how he was raised. He believes God has gotten him this far in life. He believes that God played a major part in helping him make it to college. He believes that God helped his mother find a way to raise him and his brother as a single mom when their father wasn't there," I said. "I understand, but at the same time, I hope that eventually, he will realize that for God to be love, you have to treat everyone with love, and that your actions have to show that love, especially where family is concerned."

Less than a year later, Chris and I would no longer be friends.

I didn't see it. Didn't see his anger, didn't see his pride, didn't see the envy in his eyes. Yes, all of us were friends. Yes, we all liked one another. However, as Chris would state later, some within our circle held more esteem than others. Some birthdays were celebrated in higher fashion, some friends kept secrets from others, some gatherings were arranged without notifying certain friends ahead of time. I participated in the exclusion—and I liked it. I liked having secrets with others that even those within our small circle didn't know. I liked that on my birthday everyone came to surprise me in the lobby, greeting me with a handmade cake and a personalized card decorated with glitter and coated with nice words about what my friendship meant to each individual who signed it. I liked being included, and part of me liked when others weren't. It made me feel special, as if I was more important.

I did not realize or care that Chris felt as if he was the odd man out, that he wasn't given the same attention other friends were. I did not realize that Chris had already lost respect for me, that our friendship was already over.

Chapter 23: Losing

"All you do is talk about people!" Chris said loudly. "That's all you do!"

"Chris, you know you get mad, too," I said testily.

"Mad when? You mean when you told Bernadette how much better you were than me in Madden when you thought I wasn't listening?" He said incredulously.

"Chris, that's not even what happened," I said in an attempt to reestablish some calm but which came off more like a whine."

"You really think you know everything!" Chris said loudly. "But all you do is talk behind people's backs! You did it with Madden, and you did it with other stuff, too—that's all you do!"

"Uhhh! I'm so sick of you mentioning that Madden game! It happened a year ago!" I groaned, thrashing my hands up and down violently. Chris mimicked me, gesticulating widely, his hands and arms waving in front of his body.

"What's good?" Chris shouted.

"Stop bringing up the same shit!" I retorted. "You don't know what you're talking about. You never do," I said coldly.

"Oh, really? Let's go, then!" Chris shouted, putting his fists up.

"I'm not gonna hit you first, but if you try to hit me I will come at you," I said determinedly.

"You're waving your hands around!" Chris said. "You must want to fight!"

"I'm not gonna fight you, Chris," I said, sighing. "And neither are you, we're in the middle of the cafeteria and we'll both get expelled. If you wanted to do something you would have done it already."

"You scared?" You scared?" I'll do it, I don't care!" Chris said vehemently.

"Go ahead then!" I shouted at Chris, angrier still. "Go ahead then! Do it!" I hollered. Chris hesitated then moved toward me before being held back by Jessie. "Let's go," Jessie said to Chris, pulling him to the side.

"C'mon man, c'mon," someone said to me, holding me back as I stood in the same spot I had for the past 5 minutes. I complied slowly, drawing my shoulders up in a more relaxed stance before departing. I walked back to my dorm, angry, this time at myself. I had lost my temper, shouting belligerently in front of a crowd of people. I might as well have stripped off my beige suit right there.

No one who witnessed my outburst could have seen how hard I worked in school, drilling myself constantly on the phrases and concepts I needed to remember for the upcoming midterm. No one could have seen how respectful I was to the women in my life, doting on them whenever I could. Indeed, all they saw was the disturbed man shouting in front of them, and there was nothing I could do to change that. The color of my skin should not have mattered. But unfortunately, it did. It mattered the minute I decided to act out the long-held stereotype of the angry, loud, in-your-face, black man. I was the man non-black students were wary of interacting with for the first time when they went off to school. I was the man who was just lucky to escape his urban environment. I was seen as the token, the Affirmative Action case, the athlete and the class clown, the possible thief, the hustler.

I was the man black students' parents had warned their children to stay away from for fear of guilt by association. I was the person who black students scoffed at with their friends, the "nigga" the *nigger.* I was the man they had to hide from, for fear of tarnishing their own beige suits, those pieces of clothing worn to cover a less accepted version of themselves No one could know that they too were one click away from tearing their suits. And so they shuddered when I yelled at Chris, they went back to eating and on with their lives, continuing to live above the fray, forever a member of the talented tenth, that population of blacks whom W.E.B. Du Bois claimed would be the subset responsible for obtaining good educations, for giving back to the community, for educating the nigger.

What they failed to realize, was that the talented tenth was now half the black population, the majority of whom had escaped poverty. The "nigger" was more $^{1/10}$ than 90 percent, and in reality, he had always existed in a vacuum. He was simply the ignoramus, the person who did not care about what came out of his mouth—the individual who lacked couth and refused to apologize for it. In truth, every race has one, or two, or three. But the most popular nigger still carries black skin, and it is he who will be ostracized most. It is he who will be arrested, he who will be killed.

I knew I was better than him—better tempered, better educated, better mannered. It upset me that Blacks, Asians, and whites in the room that day would mistake me for him for even a second.

As for Chris, despite how open I proclaimed to be, it was still hard for me to be friends with someone who did not share my world view. I did not have a relationship with Christ. I did not go to church every Sunday. I didn't believe there was anything wrong with two lesbians kissing on TV. I did not believe abstinence before marriage was best. I was pro-choice. Most importantly, I did not believe two gays were ill-equipped to raise a child.

Unfortunately, Chris did, and though I believed my talk with him had softened his stance, I was not naïve enough to think he had done a 180. I was more guarded with him. I failed to tell him about how great Mary was, about her seminary classes and her pro bono work for disadvantaged foster kids. I failed to tell him about Janet, who worked tirelessly to protect the rights of children, almost singlehandedly compiling cutting-edge reports on gun violence on children in America, data that would be used in textbooks for years to come. Chris did not know any of this, and because of it, my words about how great my parents were held less weight. Chris talked about his mom and the things she did all the time, but when it was my turn to talk about my family, I was eerily quiet. He may have reasoned that there were few positives for me to say about them, or that they simply did not make a big enough impact for me to speak of them in glowing terms.

I worried that after our argument, he would define my actions and words as those of someone not raised right. I worried that Mary and Janet would be blamed for their son's mistakes. When I went to apologize to Chris, my suspicions were addressed.

"Hey, man," I said, pushing his door ajar. "Can I talk to you for a minute?"

"Yeah, sure," he said blandly, turning away from his computer. I waited for him to speak, but when he remained silent I realized that it was still my turn.

"So, I just wanted to let you know that I am sorry for what I said before." I said. "I really didn't mean to get angry, and I was not trying to fight you or punk you in any way—I was just upset when you mentioned me talking about people—and, you're right, I do talk about people too much. It's just that last year, when the Madden game thing happened, I really did not go around telling people I beat you, it really wasn't important to me. Bernadette just happened to ask me who won, and went around telling people you were mad I guess—I have told you that's how it happened before, and was just frustrated that it didn't sink in."

"I understand that," Chris said. "But honestly, it's not even about that—you said a lot of things," he said slowly.

"I honestly started to lose respect for you a while ago," he added. "People in the group have been coming up to me telling me to apologize or to forgive you after our argument—but I'm not going to do that just for the sake of the group," he said defiantly. "I think it's messed up that even within the group there are small cliques… I think it's messed up that certain birthdays are celebrated more. Like, when Ant's birthday came up, no one really did anything, so I got him a card, and went to his room—no one else did anything—so I'm just sick of it," he said in a matter of fact tone. "And when you did this (mimics me thrusting my hands up and down), you were threatening me—like, you wanted to fight. The only way we could be cool now—like, is if we were to fight, and *maybe* then everything would be cool, but that's not even worth it.

"I mean honestly, I think it goes back to us being raised differently—I was raised to always respect other people," he said pointedly. "I was raised to include other people, I was raised to believe that if you had something to say to someone, you said it to their face," he said passionately.

"I know your parent's lifestyle was different, and that's okay. But—yeah man, I just can't be friends with someone like that.

"It doesn't mean that I'm mad—because I'm not—but as far as chilling together in the crew, and talking and stuff like that, it's just not gonna happen… I'll still be cordial with you when I see you, and I won't hold a grudge, but that's it."

His voice came to a halt as I looked on, slightly dumbfounded. "All right, man," I said wearily, "if that's what you want... I don't hold any grudges, and respect that—I'm glad you were honest.

"I've always respected how you spoke of your mom, and don't know exactly what you mean by 'lifestyle' in referring to my parents, but I was raised right. If I make a mistake, I make sure to take responsibility, and to correct it. I was taught that everyone makes mistakes, and that it's important to be able to forgive." I said. "But like I said, I respect that you were honest— anyway, take care, man," I said. I quickly retreated from the room without shaking his hand. Chris looked on without speaking, a frown on his face.

The trip back to my dorm was short, as Chris's room was only one floor down from mine. I walked to the end of the hall and made my way up the narrow staircase. I inhaled quickly, gathering myself after reaching the top step, slowly pushing open the red door leading to Patapsco South. I walked past two brown doors before spotting a sign inches from the white ceiling emblazoned with the number "112." I calmly unlocked my door and trudged in, tossing my keys on the cord-littered nightstand. I opened my fridge and grabbed a peach yogurt before plopping on my big, blue chair. I ripped open the yogurt container, squirting several orange drops on my polo shirt. I flicked them away absentmindedly as I analyzed Chris's words.

I had told him that I did not hold grudges, and that forgiveness was important, but I was finding it hard to accept what he had said. I had expected him to apologize, to want to be friends again. Being anything less would affect not only us, but our friends as well. It would force members of our group to hang out with Chris or me exclusively, driving a wedge between everyone. Part of my apology had been for this reason alone. I was taking one for the team, and expected him to do the same. I had already gotten over our fight. Nothing Chris had said during our argument was harsh enough for me to dismiss him. My anger had lasted for several days, but was hard to hold onto. I had expected him to feel the same way. However after speaking with him, it was evident that he had moved past the point of anger, and into the territory of resentment. He just… didn't like me—which felt weird. The prospect of him and I never being friends again had crossed my mind, but the idea of us not being friends because he did not think I was a good enough person to form a bond with was hard to digest.

    I no longer looked at myself as innocent or righteous. That space had been replaced by a confused man in denial. A man in denial about his issues, and a man confused about how to overcome the darkness he felt inside him. I had been depressed for years, but I had always thought I hid it well. As I sank into my comfy chair, I realized that I had spent more energy trying to conceal my pain than finding ways to address it. Somewhere along the way showing others how tough I was had become more important than finding inner peace. Somewhere along the line I had convinced myself that I didn't need peace at all.

I scraped the last peach chunk from the bottom of the cup, folding the container in my hand and setting it in the full kitchen-sized trash bag by the fridge.

I contemplated my next move, struggling with my catharsis. The source of my trepidation came not in the fact that I had discovered that I was failing to cover my pain, but that I was no closer to finding out how to get rid of it.

Chris's words *"we were raised differently"* and *"your parents lived a different lifestyle"* stuck with me. It was as if my behavior had confirmed everything he already knew about same-sex-headed households. It had been my job to be the flag bearer for our family, and I had dropped it.

I realized that day that I was wearing a completely different type of suit, one that covered not my race, but my familial background. Every time I did the right thing, and every time I spoke well, I kept the new suit on. Every time I lashed out, and every time I wronged someone close to me, I ripped it.

The purpose of the suit was to cover the fact that I was raised by gay parents, while managing to acknowledge how great a person I was *because* I was raised by gay parents—a delicate but doable task. The only way the suit could be damaged was if I negatively represented myself. To do that was to misrepresent my moms as well. Any action I took, negative or positive, was always a reflection of them. Taken as a whole, my actions defined their character just as much as they did mine.

Each child raised in a same-sex household becomes an example—an example for a specific type of family dynamic, an example for a state of mind, and in many ways—a stereotype. Because stereotypes inform how we think about populations we have little contact with, and because the average person will not meet an inordinate number of children raised by gays, first impressions remain vital. Friendships are even more important, for they allow the child of gay parents to form a deeper bond with a peer, a bond which can make it easier to understand the viewpoint of someone raised within a household different from his or her own. Above all, forming friendships allows peers to see the child of the same-sex couple as an individual, a man or woman capable of making his or her own decisions.

My argument with Chris, and our subsequent falling out, had robbed us of the chance to form a deeper bond, and had robbed him of an opportunity to learn more about me as an individual. I worried that I had blown a golden opportunity to change the mind of someone opposed to gay adoption, to form an ally who could relate to others that they knew a child of a same-sex couple; an ally who could state that I had faults, but was dedicated to correcting them. An ally who could tell people that I cared about others, that I was humble—that I loved my parents.

I now knew that Chris was not that ally, and that convincing people that the same sex-headed household was just as righteous a home as the heterosexual-headed one would be harder than I thought. There was still a faction of the population who felt like Chris, and who thought gays were unfit to raise children. Until that faction was reduced to zero, I had to continue to befriend people who shared his views. The task was harder than it looked, but possible nevertheless. I had lost one friendship, but there were more Chris's out there. More people ready to change. When that time came, I would be ready, because I had been raised to never give up—and not just on myself.

Chapter 24: She's in Hell

I shuffled through an already cracked door, smiling at them before grabbing an uncomfortable chair by the window. A "thud" was heard as the chair was set unceremoniously on the coffee-stained carpet. I looked up to see if they cared and received… nothing, not even a glance. They were too busy in their own conversation to notice there were four walls in the room, let alone an extra chair by their feet. They came out of their reverie long enough to ask me my opinion on the important subject they were discussing. "I don't know, man," I said—I think Kobe is better right now." See! Told you," one of them said. "Man, whatever," the other said, "I'll take LeBron any day over him." "Blasphemous," I chimed in. "LeBron hasn't earned his spot yet." "Whatever, man," he said. You're crazy."

"But yeah, man…" he said, changing subjects. "You talked to Chris?"

"Yeah I spoke with him," I said.

"How'd it go?" he asked.

"It didn't go too well, Dayo, didn't go too well." I said, trailing off.

"You two will find a way to squash this," he said. "It'll just take time."

"Nah, I don't think so, man," I said.

"Damn, really?" Dayo said.

"Yeah, man," I said.

"I mean, listen," he said, "Chris told me what happened and I can understand why he was mad. He felt like you disrespected him by stepping to him the way you did.

"The words you used may not have been that bad, but you're tone is not correct sometimes, I remember one time you said this to me," he said as I zoned out, waiting for him to come back to his point. "So when you said that stuff to Chris," he said, finally done, "you probably came at him in a disrespectful way—you see what I mean?"

"Yeah," I said tepidly.

"So when you spoke that way to him and then did this (gesticulates me waving my right arm up and down in a frustrated manner) Chris felt like you were trying to punk him in front of all those people. So—see what I'm saying?" Dayo said wisely.

"Yeah, I understand that," I said. "And yeah sometimes my tone could be better. But, honestly, I feel like Chris hasn't been cool with me for a while, and the argument was just a reason for him to be able to write me off."

"Why do you say that?" Dayo asked.

"I just think," I said, hesitating, "that Chris has a problem with the way I was raised."

"Why?" Dayo said. I paused, debating whether or not I wanted to say the words that lingered on my mind.

I started. "So—I was adopted by two women who happened to be lesbians," I said calmly. I waited for Dayo to interject, and when he did not, continued. "Chris knows this— because I told him. At the time, I thought he was cool with it. However, when I talked to him the other day he said that part of the reason he wasn't willing to patch things up is because we just weren't raised the same."

I looked at Dayo, whose eyes belied a man in intense thought. He looked at the wall, then at an adjacent desk, before turning to address me.

"I mean, for real," Dayo said. "I can understand why Chris might not have fucked with you because of who you were raised by. I mean listen, they raised you, did a great job, played a great role. But you should look at your situation as a blessing from God. Like, how many people who were in your position are where you are right now? How many of those kids in your orphanage weren't even adopted? God has a plan for you," he said. "At every stage in your life, he put people in front of you who would set you on the right path.

"Look at where you are," he said, motioning to the rest of the room. "You are a college-educated black man in America. That alone makes you lucky—the fact that you were adopted should make it clear that you were more than just lucky.

"But," he said abruptly. "You should realize that your adoptive parents are nothing more than people God placed in your life. They helped you, but that does not mean you have to defend the lifestyle they lead." he said. "God says that homosexuality is wrong," he said, swiping a Bible off the desk.

"Look—right here… Leviticus," he said, quoting the specific book in the Old Testament. "Lying with mankind as with womankind: it is an abomination," he read aloud, closing the Bible abruptly.

"There! You see?" He said passionately. "It's right there for you. I'm sorry. This isn't something that's debatable. Your moms are going to hell. It's a fact," he said. I looked up at him, a glint in my eye and a word on my tongue.

"Fact?" I asked inquisitively. "Why is it 'fact'?"

"Because God expressly says that homosexuality is a sin, and that gay people are going to hell," Dayo responded.

"See, that's where we have a difference of opinion," I said. "You believe that God said that—I don't."

"Explain," Dayo said.

"Man wrote those words, not God," I said. "To me, God is love, and God condemning an entire group of people to Hell just because of who they sleep with, doesn't make sense to me."

"Of course you would say that," Dayo interjected, "you were raised by two women."

"Yes," I said, "I was. And because of that I have a unique perspective. I got to see my moms interacting with each other every day, striving to do the right thing. They are great people."

"No one is saying they aren't great people," Dayo replied slyly. "They are obviously nice people, good people, who gave you a home and made you the man you are today. That is not what I'm disputing," he said, clearing his throat. "What I'm saying is that that doesn't mean that they are not sinning."

"Think of it like this," he said. "It's like a drug addict. They may be a great person, but they continue to sin and sin and sin—every day. But—if they repent and stop sinning, then they have a chance of going to Heaven. The difference with gay people," he said, pausing for effect. "Is that what they do, who they are, **is a perpetual sin**. The very lifestyle they lead is sin. So for them, there isn't saving in the way that there is for the drug addict."

"If they continue to lead that lifestyle up until the day they die, they are going to hell, and it's as plain as that—regardless of how great they were."

I looked at Dayo, annoyed, but ready to respond. Despite what he had said, I still viewed our conversation as a debate. I cued up my voice and began. "I do not believe that," I said confidently. "Everyone has different beliefs, and I'm not trying to change yours."

"I'm not trying to change yours either," Dayo said. "I'm just telling you facts. Your two moms did a great job, and I'm sure they are perfectly nice people. Like—what do they do for a living?" he asked genuinely.

"Well," I said. "Janet works for the Children's Defense Fund, an organization that stands up for the rights of kids. Mary passed away in 2001, but she was a lawyer for kids represented in family court, as well as a professor."

"I'm sorry to hear that," Dayo interjected sadly. "I'm glad she spent her life helping people, though.

"But even that," he said passionately, "is God showing you a sign. Mary's purpose in life was to raise you, to hone the man you would become."

I nodded slightly before responding. "Mary was a great woman. And she was great long before I came into the picture. She spent her entire life helping other people," I said. "And she would have done that whether or not I was her son," I added.

"Your version of God and my version of God is different," I said. "Your version of God would put a great woman—a great person, in Hell. I cannot accept that. I cannot believe in any religion that accepts that, either.

"However," I said, "I believe in *my* version of God, which is how I know that Mary is in Heaven. I know that the God I believe in, the God who places love and altruism first, took Mary to a better place after she died. That's really all it is to me."

"I respect that you think that," Dayo said. "But you have to admit that if you were raised by other people, anyone else, that your beliefs would be different."

"Of course they would be different," I said. "Who you are raised by plays a big part in anyone's belief system. I would like to think that I would still believe that there was nothing wrong with being gay regardless of who I was raised by, but I cannot say that for sure."

"However, to be honest," I said. "That is irrelevant. I believe what I believe. That's not going to change—ever. Mary will always be in Heaven, and good people will always be rewarded in the end."

"That is what I believe, and that is how I was raised. It's who I am," I said. "And if you were raised by gay people, your mindset might be different."

"My mindset wouldn't be different," Dayo said, "because being gay to me is something that is inherently wrong."

"But," I said. "You learned that from somewhere. You didn't just wake up one day and say *'Hey, you know what? Being gay isn't cool.'* Who you were raised by influenced your train of thought. That is why I don't attack your beliefs."

"You know—I wish they were different," I said. "But I understand that that is how you were raised, and that because of that, you hold a specific set of morals that are unique to you. It's the same for me—my views are just different. If you could see our family—how normal we are, how we operate on a daily basis, maybe those views would change. But for now, let's just say that you have your beliefs, and I have mine.

"Don't say or suggest that my moms are going to Hell though," I said. "I understand what you believe, and I respect that. But if you say something like that in my presence again, we will have problems," I said respectfully.

"Okay," Dayo said. "Respect," he added, shaking my hand. "The main thing, man, is that God has a plan for you. Just remember that," he said, looking me in the eye. "I'll pray for you."

"Thanks," I said forlornly, disappointed as I turned and walked from the room, my shoulders feeling heavier than when I entered. I walked a few paces, turned to my left, and faced my dorm room, twisting the knob slowly before pushing the door open. It creaked loudly then banged lightly against the white wall. I threw my keys on the desk and took a seat in front of my clunky laptop. I reflected on every word that was said, every eye twitch, every hand movement. Dayo's words had affected me, but it was my own that I thought the most about.

I had spoken not only of my moms, but of Mary's death as well, a subject normally addressed in the company of my closet friends. Bringing it up in front of someone that was not that was—out of the norm, but not difficult in and of itself. She had been dead 8 years at the time. However, speaking of her death to make an argument to defend an overarching point about the viability of the gay-headed household had not been something I had ever imagined I would be doing. Saying that "she was not in Hell," was never something I imagined having to say. But there it was, in plain sight. I had brought it up, and I had decided to discuss it.

Dayo was a talker, an intellectual. His views were misguided, but I doubted he would change them. He was just as convinced in his beliefs as Chris had been, but was more passionate about expressing how they had come to be, about how God had set a path for him. I was too tired to worry about ways I could change a mind that for the time being was set in stone. The only thing I had energy for was remembering Mary—my best friend, my first soccer training partner. As for Dayo's "Hell" comments, I knew they would not hurt me in the long run because I had already endured the toughest thing life had ever offered me. Living through that gave me perspective on the difference between miniscule words, and a real problem. My nightmare had already come true, my conversation with him had only brought it to light. I sat there in the dark, reflecting on Dayo's words, and then painting pictures with my own. *"She passed away, 2001, she was great."* The words attached themselves to images of the day I would never forget—the day Mary died.

Chapter 25: Death

It was a Thursday, the penultimate day of an otherwise uneventful work week. It was hot, one of those muggy, humid, sweat-drenched late June days that make you long for one more day of frigid, February air. I had worked all day honing my skills at soccer camp, a pair of black Puma cleats on my feet and a shirt with a small *Nike* logo on my chest. Sweat dripped from my temple to my neck as I took my last few shots on net. I wiped my brow before sauntering off the field as a dull pain invaded my forehead. I touched the end line and walked over to the water cooler, reaching down to grab a white plastic cup as I pressed down on a black lever. The water drained from the cooler at my will as I held the cup steady, drawing it up to my nose when I was ready.

I took one sip, then splashed the rest of the water on my face in direct protest of my screaming, dehydrated body. The water dripped from my jersey and onto the blistering turf as I picked my tennis shoes up and walked off the field before making my way into an empty parking lot. I stood there for a few moments, looking to and fro for the blue Subaru I knew was sure to come. Thirty seconds later it arrived, its blue hood shining in the harsh sunlight. It made a left then swerved into an adjacent parking spot before coming to a complete stop. The driver's side door opened as Janet stepped out of it, her salt and pepper shoulder-length hair catching the gleaming light. She walked a few paces forward, leaving her door open as she made eye contact with me, her eyes soft behind a set of corrective glasses. I hobbled towards her, my body moving like that of a linebacker past his prime. I glanced at Janet, her slumping shoulders giving me pause. She moved shuffled towards me as I moved closer, my legs moving sloppily one after the other, trying to gather a momentum that failed to come. After several painful seconds I arrived at my destination, but Janet failed to greet me. Instead she hesitated for a couple moments before speaking, sighing once.

"Mama died," she said—"early this morning." I was angry. *Why hadn't anyone told me?* I thought. *Why hadn't I been informed of Mama's death when it happened? Why hadn't Janet brought me to the hospital last night so I could stay with Mama before she passed away?* As my temper died down though, all I could think of was—*"That's the news?"*

"That's all she had to tell me? That was not news, I told myself. *That was expected.* Mama had been given 2 days to live 4 days ago. Her passing was not a question of *if,* but *when.* I looked at Janet, then walked over to the passenger side, brusquely opening and closing the door before plopping myself down on a jelly-stained car seat. Janet climbed into the car slowly, starting the car before shifting the clutch to drive, her neck swiveling from side to side as she checked for oncoming traffic. The car bumped awkwardly over a divot as we made our way past a worn-down stop sign and onto a main road. I looked anywhere but at Janet, who glanced at me out of the corner of her eye, turning her gaze back to the road when she realized I would not return her gaze. We passed some buildings, and some fields, but nothing made an impression. It took around 20 minutes to get home and Janet and I spent it just sitting there, the sound of the purring air conditioner the only thing that cut into our ever-expanding thoughts. The car rolled to a stop as Janet put the car in park, taking the keys out of the ignition and opening her door without a word. She stepped out of the car awkwardly, carving a path to the door as I lagged behind, patiently waiting for her to take out her keys. She reached in her left pocket, fumbling a bit before snatching them up. They dangled in the light as she flipped several one over the other before finding the one she was looking for. She inhaled, then screwed the key in.

Our mangy mutt Harriet shuffled at the foot of the doorway as she eagerly awaited her owners, sniffing at Janet's jacket as we made our way through the doorway. I took off my cleats and sat down on the living room couch.

"We are still out of hot water," Janet said. "Martha has offered to let us shower at her house," Janet said, "I have told her you will be coming up there when you are ready."

"Ok," I said solemnly. I ran upstairs, stripping off a pair of dirt-stained socks before putting on a set of old cross trainers. I walked to the bathroom, grabbing a yellow loofa wash cloth and a half-empty bottle of body wash, before going downstairs, where I was met by Janet.

"Remember to thank Martha," she said calmly. I nodded, then walked out of the house, trudging up the steep hill that led to Martha's house. I rounded the narrow corner, and then made my way up to her walkway. Her silhouette stood by the doorway as I inched closer, unsure of myself. I hesitated, debating whether or not to knock or open the door, when it swung open, revealing a pink-faced Martha. She greeted me with open arms and directed me to the upstairs bathroom. She didn't say a word, but the sadness written on her face spoke volumes. I nodded curtly then marched up the stairs, slipping into a bathroom located next to Martha's bedroom. I closed the door, staring at the pane glass shower cover, which distorted my face into a set of grey pixels. I looked away from it and stripped off my clothes, dumping them in a heap beside the toilet. I turned on the shower, took off my soccer shorts, and stepped into the warm shower.

The water washed over me as salt from the hard-fought day fell at my feet and raced to the drain. I closed my eyes and thought of Mary, beginning to whimper. One tear fell, then two, then three. Another fell as I struggled to take in the situation surrounding me. It almost felt as if I was willing myself to cry. As if I needed to act in accordance with the situation. However, crying seemed to make me more depressed, snapshots of Mary's mile wide smile presenting themselves. I twisted the faucet, the water turning from a steady stream to a light trickle. I reached to my left blindly, clawing at a floral towel. I dried off slowly, dabbing the mixture of tap water and tears that lingered on my cheeks. I tiptoed across the room, snagging a pair of underwear and jeans I had brought from home. They clung to my damp body as I put each article on. I ignored how uncomfortable it felt, picking up a pair of wrinkled socks off the floor.

My pruned, clammy feet welcomed the dry piece of clothing, coating my body in fleeting warmth. I turned to the toilet, swiping an old T-shirt off the seat. I adjusted it to make sure it fit perfectly. I patted my shoulders and chest to make sure there were no wrinkles. I gave up; losing myself in the jagged corn maze I called my shirt. I turned to my left, reaching for a black set of tennis shoes located under a heap of dirty clothes. I plucked them up with my right pinky, flinging a pair of grass-stained shorts to the side with a free hand. I carefully placed the shoes on my feet and tied the trainers with extra care, making sure every knot was tied **just** right. After my task was finished, after the shoes were tied, the pants buttoned, the T-shirt safely on my back, my mind shifted back to reality. There was nothing left to do… and I had no idea what to do next.

Chapter 26: Funeral

The tumors had metastasized to her liver, that's what they said. There was nothing they could do. She was gone. It was hard, knowing that. Knowing she would never come back to us. A part of me had trouble believing it. Even with her elongated hospital stays, even with her emaciated, jaundiced skin, I had believed she would make it. But she had not, and now here we were—here I was.

I was not lost, but I was stranded. I spent most of my days in my room, the door shut, the curtains drawn, music blaring in my ears. The weeks became a complete blur, the only clear sound coming from Janet's far away voice on the phone. "Yes." "Thanks." "Okay," she said wearily, trying to field over 50 calls and answering 100 doorbells in the weeks following Mary's death. I hid in my room most of the time, coming down to thank the well-wishers for their fruit basket, but only if they saw my shadow through the window as I tried to sneak back upstairs.

When they left I breathed a sigh of relief, returning to my room to sulk. The scenario played itself out day after day, right up until Mary's memorial service.

It was silent in the house that day, the meowing of a hunger-deprived cat one of the only sounds to be heard. It was a hot early July day, just 3 weeks after Mary's death. I woke up with a bead of sweat on my forehead, still finding it hard to realize that Mary was not coming back. It felt as though she would appear in the doorway any second, wearing that same toothy grin she always wore. The other part of me though, the part conscious of each button my ashy hand tightened on my crisp blue dress shirt, realized that that was impractical. That part of me looked in the mirror, happy at how good its body looked in its junior grey suit. That part of me was excited for the day's events, excited to see all of my friends in the same place.

Janet came in the room, keys in hand, dressed in a dark blue blouse, grey suit, ready to depart. I followed her out the door, making sure my shoes were tied. We huddled into a cluttered car, neither of us wishing to speak. Ten minutes later, we were at the chapel. I looked down as we stopped, glaring at a sweaty palm that had as much to do with heat as it did nerves. I wiped it off on my suit pants, pushing the car door open. Janet pushed her door open simultaneously as we rose out of the SUV. Within a few steps, we were greeted by many familiar, smiling faces.

After speaking briefly with each of them, we made our way up the old marble steps and into the old grey chapel. We were seated in the front row as the pastor directed everyone in the audience to be seated. What was said in her opening remarks appear to me like a muted black and white film. I must have zoned out, either too bored or too tired to genuinely perk up. I cruised on autopilot through the rest of the service, looking back from time to time to catch a glimpse of some of my friends in the audience as the rest of the congregation sung a hymn with words I didn't know.

I was pleased, the service was going pretty well and I hadn't had to lift a finger. I looked at our pastor, her voice jovial as she introduced person after person, each with their own Mary story to tell. That day I learned that Mary was a great, if unorganized college roommate, the hardest-nosed rugby player on her team, and a caring teacher to her college students. She was a writer, a thinker, and the strongest person in the room, "even if that room had a few dads in it", one scrawny man joked. The whole crowd was laughing, a far cry from the tears and sadness I had imagined before the day began. I allowed my mind to wander off once again, this time to what kind of pizza I would have later. "*Pepperoni*" I thought to myself. The service continued as visions of sticky cheese clouded my mind, my stomach beginning to growl. *I'm getting ahead of myself,* I thought*, the service isn't even half over.* I peered back up at the pulpit, determined to focus for at least a few minutes. In my time away, the pastor had gotten serious, her words escape me, but her tone does not. It was low, gravely, pointed. She looked right, then left, pausing before each word, sighing before each sentence. Suddenly she glanced in my direction, her face pink with emotion. "And if Mary were here…" she began to say, contemplating how to best word her next sentence.

"Tony," she said in a trembling voice, finding herself. "Mary loved you *so much*. If she were here today she would be so proud of you, she will *always* be with you.

"And if she were here today," she said, picking up where she left off. "She would tell you to keep going, to get good grades in school—to be the man she knows you are destined to be. She will always be with you," she uttered, the vowel in "you" hanging in the air for what seemed like hours. I looked up at her sheepishly, attempting to find the correct body language.

I wanted my face to remain strong, but it crumbled under the light. I looked down at my feet, contemplating absolutely… nothing. I felt the eyes of the entire congregation on me, their gaze burning a hole in my back. I suddenly felt hot, a bead of sweat forming on my forehead. I knew everyone was still staring at me, but I refused to acknowledge them, caught up in my own torment. Every word that had been uttered, every inflection in her voice, started to convert themselves into images of Mary: her smile, her laugh, her blue eyes, her curly hair. *Mary played with me in the backyard, failed to catch fish on our camping trip, passed out bananas at a soccer game.*

It was all too much, too difficult to think about. I waited until the next hymn began, and then walked into the hall, determined not to cry in front of anyone. I moved through a dim light and down an adjacent staircase, kneeling on the last step. In the darkness I began to lose myself, tears bouncing off an old floor. It seemed to last forever—the crying, the heavy breathing, the exhaustion. I never wanted it to stop. I wanted to let it all out until it was gone, until the pain passed. I cried and cried, refusing to hold back. Suddenly though, I felt as if I should. I was looking down, my eyes composed on the water leaking from the two brown pools below my eyelashes—but I felt it.

I felt another pair of eyes lurking in the darkness. I tried to put my guard back up, failing. The tears just kept on coming, irreversible now. I looked up, my eyesight blurry. A golden light washed down on my tear-soaked face as a figure appeared at the top of the stairs. I wiped a glob of water from my face, wondering whose eyes were gazing into mine. My vision sharpened and there she was in full view, a frown on her face and a tissue in her hand. Rikki just stood there, motionless. Her eyes waded into my soul. I slowly raised my shoulders, attempting to exude a confidence that had eluded me. I was in front of the girl of my dreams, and here I was, crying like a toddler. I wanted to hide, to run away in shame. I wanted to wipe Rikki's mind, to force her to forget she ever saw me in such pain. However, Rikki looked as though she understood. She understood that she wasn't supposed to see me like this. She understood that she was invading my privacy. She understood that I would not want to talk about this later. Still, she continued to stand there because she knew how much Mary had meant to me, it dawning on her for perhaps the first time. She knew that I needed a friend, that I needed her. She also knew that I needed to be alone, which is why she left, casting a dark shadow as she left. I looked up, a part of me wishing she would have stayed just a little longer, looked at me just one more time.

Her sudden arrival tempered me, my breathing more shallow than it had been minutes before. Suddenly I realized that I was sick of crying. I slowly drew myself up to full height, absentmindedly wiping a wet cheek. I took a deep breath, walking back up the pale steps, feeling more like myself. I reached the top then walked back through the small hallway, bracing myself for the rest of the day.

I took my seat quietly, and without much fanfare, as the pastor went back to doing her sermon thing. I zoned out until the service was over, shaking hands with the throng of people who greeted Janet and me as we moved from aisle to aisle. After shaking hands with a particularly large man I spotted Devin and Pat, who posed in the hall, waiting for their friend to join them. I said goodbye to the man and then made a beeline to them, exiting at the same door I had wandered in a half hour earlier. "Hey, man," Devin said in an even voice.

"Hey," I said back sheepishly.

"Wow, look at how many people are here," Pat said loudly. "I don't even know half of them."

"Yeah," Devin said redundantly, "there are a lot of people here."

"Yeah, didn't expect this many people," I said.

"Mary was *definitely* more popular than you are," Pat said. Devin and I chuckled, waiting for each other to speak. I broke the silence first.

"All right—well, I'm about ready to leave," I said.

"All right, cool," Devin said, "let's roll out." We moved past an old couple, spotting our parents talking to one another in front of the church fountain. I moved first, rudely interrupting an adult conversation.

"Mom," I said flatly. "I'm gonna head out with Dev and Pat now." I said it with such confidence, as if I had the car keys in my hands.

"Okay," Janet said. "Call from their house when you get there."

"Okay," I said shortly, turning on my heel to rejoin Devin and Pat. "Okay, we're good," I said.

"All right, let's do it." Devin said quickly as we made our way down a set of chapel steps toward the car.

"Dad!" Pat yelled, "we're ready."

"Ya ready, man?" Dennis replied in his northeastern drawl.

"Yup," I said shyly.

"All right, let's go, then." Dennis said. We walked past the prayer garden and down the street before reaching their blue sedan. Dennis opened the door for Laurie as Devin, Pat, and I piled in the backseat. Pat was the last one to slam his door shut behind him as Dennis revved the engine. The car whirred, and we were off.

The car remained silent for an awkward moment, with no one sure exactly how to break the tension. It was Pat who spoke up first. "Hey," he said. "Wasn't that *so rude* of the pastor to say that to you?" He asked somewhat rhetorically. "Like—her doing that is exactly the opposite of what Mary would have wanted."

"Yeah," Devin said, "I was thinkin' that, too. That was ridiculous. Like, *Hey Tony, I know you must feel so, so bad right now, like, let me make you feel like some absolute shit,"* Devin chimed in, mocking the pastors voice.

"Yeah, I didn't like that either," Laurie said awkwardly.

"I mean it wasn't like everyone in the church didn't know that," Pat said. "There was completely no need for her to be overdramatic like that."

We ditched the adults a few minutes later and spent the rest of the day relaxing and playing video games, crashing at around 2:00 a.m. It was around 3:00 a.m. when we realized none of us were asleep. The three of us sat up, alert as could be. Devin and Pat told me that they loved me, and that whatever I needed, they would be there to provide. None of us really knew how we would process Mary's death, about how we would respond. But they knew that for me, the process would be especially hard, and that they would need to be there to lend a helping hand when I needed one. It was a hard task to ask of a couple of adolescent boys, but they were willing to take up the post. "We got your back," Devin said proudly, looking me dead in the eye. I looked back, knowing that his statement was true.

"Thanks, guys," I said. "I really appreciate that." We turned off the lights, finally going to sleep—Pat flailing on the floor as he tried to get comfortable in a heap of blankets, Devin tossing and turning on his bed. I settled into a comfortable spot on my side, hugging my sleeping bag tight to my body, thoughts still racing. *Mary was Devin and Pat's first soccer coach, too,* I thought to myself. *She made pasta for them on a random Wednesday night as well, went camping with them in the summer as well.* I turned back over, my eyes finally closing.

***

In each family, death hits each member differently. One member may feel sad. Another may feel angry. Another may feel distant. I felt all three. I didn't want people around me, because I felt the loss was something only I could go through. I felt angry because Mary had been taken from me. I had been robbed. I had been granted two loving parents only to lose one of them. I would have to live the rest of my life without one of my best friends. I would have to keep looking people in the eye and telling them I was okay when I wasn't. It was comforting to know that with Devin and Pat, I could be weak if I wanted to. I had spent the last few weeks trying to be so strong that I had forgotten that part of strength was acknowledging the need to be weak.

Chapter 27: Dealing

It was funny how Mary's death changed our family dynamic. There were stares when we went out now, but they weren't gawking. There were questions asked at school, but there were not conversations. It was freeing in some ways, the end of a burden. Janet dropped me off at school every day and people just assumed. They assumed she was my mother, or foster parent, or stepmom, or grandmom. No one asked me about how it was growing up, or had questions about Mary's cancer. I was free to simply roam, to live above the ruckus. I enjoyed it. I enjoyed not having to deal with it anymore. I enjoyed not having to go to a hospital I hated. I enjoyed not having to be the kid with two moms.

However, I was ashamed of myself, ashamed for distancing myself from Mary, from her legacy. It was too easy for me to cover who I really was, and I knew that somewhere, Mary was watching me. I imagined her hating me. Hating me for every omission, every side-stepping of the conversation of gays in America. Every time I had had a chance to defend my moms and declined. Every time I failed to mention her death. Every time I failed to mention her life. It was all there, a book with which she could beat me to death.

All those years, my moms had taught me to stand up for myself, and to stand up for those I cared about. I had treated Mary's death as if it had exempted me from those tasks. Even the way I talked of her death covered the fact of who she was to me. "My mom died," I would say. Failing to explain *which* mom had died, *which* mom was no longer with me.

It was cowardly, and unfair not only to Mary, but to Janet as well. She was the mom still with me every day. She still picked me up after school every weekday, and took me to soccer games every weekend. She was still there every time I cried out at night. To deny part of who Mary was to me was to deny what Janet was to me as well.

The sad part is that I knew that; I knew what I was doing, but continued to do it anyway. It was as if taking the easy way out drained me of at least some of the burden of Mary's death—as if it had granted me this positive thing, this ability to be normal. I thought that was what normal was: *positive.* I thought that different was negative. All of the books I had read had taught me that. The history lessons I learned in third grade had taught me that. Everyone that was different seemed to get killed, or ostracized, or segregated. And everyone who was different seemed to get talked about. I was tired of being talked about. I was tired of being talked to. I had no more to say. Sometimes I wondered if Janet felt it, too—the end of a burden. I would never ask her aloud, but the thought continued to cross my mind. She had been there for Mary for years, had taken care of seeing to it that Mary got to the hospital safe and sound for the past 5 years, all while raising me. It had to be difficult. It *was* difficult. Maybe she felt guilty now, too. Maybe part of her felt life was easier without Mary.

Maybe she felt as though she could focus solely on her task of raising me now. I didn't really know, and Janet didn't really tell me. Her body language from day to day was consistent, as if life was just as normal as it had always been. There were no dramatic tears, no heartfelt speeches, and no angry tirades at God. Part of me felt like all of it was by design, and part of me felt as though Janet just didn't feel comfortable talking about Mary's death with me. Her demeanor was that of someone who wanted to shield others from harm at all costs, even if it meant bottling the deepest loss she had ever experienced inside.

Whatever the case, it was clear that Mary's death cast a long shadow—over both of us. It's funny when someone dies. There are so many social scripts that one is supposed to follow.

Three days of sadness followed by 4 weeks of crying followed by 2 weeks of anger followed by all of the above for intermittent parts of eternity seem to be the blueprint. For me, and for Janet, it was as if we skipped this blueprint and went straight into denial. It wasn't really a denial of Mary's death as much as it was a denial of admitting that it had affected us. We did it by not talking, and through our actions.

I remember 2 weeks after the memorial service. It was sometime in July and the sun was beating down the way it always does when a Maryland summer really kicks off. The house was just as messy as it had been the week before, but neither Janet nor I put any effort into cleaning it. Instead, we drowned our sorrows in DVDs. Whatever the genre, we were there—comedies, dramas, historical flicks, sports movies—anything we found interesting. Every Saturday was a repeat of last Saturday. We would hop in the blue Subaru and drive 35 minutes, reaching the new Best Buy by the new chain mall. We grabbed a red cart and started our journey, moving from aisle in search of movies that we didn't know we needed yet. *Remember the Titans* was put in first, followed by an old Sean Connery flick, followed by *The Simpsons*, seasons one through five. I wanted another video game, too, Madden Football was about to come out, but I wanted a shooting game, too, so we picked up James Bond, Golden Eye. I still had a PlayStation 1, so we changed that, snatching up a PlayStation 2 at full price. Janet needed her **M*A*S*H,** so we picked up every season of that, too. Every time we walked out of the store I took a peek at our receipt, with a total that seemed bigger than I had expected it to be every week. At first I felt bad, but then I remembered that this was therapy—for both of us. We needed to have a little fun. We needed to splurge a little bit. A single mom and a 12-year old do not make the most robust financial pair, but we managed to make the most of the money we had. The money that we used came from what Mary left to us. Janet had already set aside some of the money for college, and so we were left with some spending money. It didn't exactly calm everything down, but the gadgets helped me go to another place, if only for a few hours. She never said so, but I knew the same was true for Janet. She was so busy taking care of everybody else. First Mama, then me, then both of us—and she was burned out, too. I knew that she needed the gadgets just as much as I did. Her shows and her books had always been a go-to option for her. The only difference now was that she was absorbing them more than I had seen her do in the past, which was fine.

When Janet was occupied downstairs, I would sit in bed, struggling to keep my eyes open to the last *Simpson's* episode in the box set. I would falter, the room getting darker around me as my eyelids drooped. I took a blue sheet and drew it over my head, reliving the past.
Suddenly

I was flipping old Batman covers over my body, resting my head on my soft pillow as I turned over. In the distance I heard the pitter-patter of footsteps marching up the stairs, followed by the familiar creak of the brown wooden floorboards as someone made a path to my door. Yellow light flooded the room as she inched closer to my bed, unable to decipher whether or not its occupant was awake. I turned my head slowly to the left to relate that I was, at which point Mary tucked me in. By the time she was finished, I felt as though my Batman covers had morphed into some weird comic-book-sponsored straitjacket. On most nights, Mary seemed to realize this fact, too, and shifted the sheets accordingly. After she was done, she looked me in the eyes and began to recite The Lord's Prayer, at which point in time I recited the words along with her:

"Our Father, who art in heaven
Hallowed be thy Name.
Thy Kingdom come.

Thy will be done in earth,
As it is in heaven.
Give us this day our daily bread.
And forgive us our trespasses,
As we forgive them that trespass against us.
And lead us not into temptation,
But deliver us from evil.
For thine is the kingdom,
The power, and the glory,
For ever and ever.
Amen."

With that, she kissed me on the forehead, silently walking out of the room. The light flooded out of the room, and I was left to fade peacefully to sleep. I flashed back to reality, waiting for footsteps. First nothing, then a clunking sound. It grew closer and closer as I pressed my elbows into my chest, colder than I thought I was. An eerie creak was heard as a door opened. Janet stepped into the light as I pretended to be asleep. She felt my shoulders, which shivered at her touch, and then pulled my comforter off of the side of the bed, wrapping it around me until I felt as if I was in a cocoon. She picked up a fleece blanket lying on the floor and placed it over my comforter, coating me in warmth. I inhaled, releasing a stress I was unaware was there. I opened one eye briefly, catching a glimpse of her. She smiled, lost in the task she was completing. I shut my eyes quickly, doing my best to slow my breathing. She kissed me on the top of the head and walked out of the room, returning downstairs as her tennis shoes clopped on the wood floor. I drifted off to sleep, forever grateful that I was still protected by my mom.

Chapter 28: Changes

Life changes faster than expected. We have babies, move away from our parents, and start new careers. We get hit by buses, see our parents die, and divorce our spouses. We take in children, send them off to school, and develop chronic muscle aches by the time we send them off to college. Indeed, it all turns quicker than we could have imagined. The truth though, is that the changes in our lives—though fast, are rarely completely unexpected.

Being able to prepare for or expect change does not make the process any easier, though. It is still something we have to deal with. It is still something we have to live with every day. One can never prepare for being separated from their child for the first time when they go off to school, or waking up to find the body print of their former lover not still impressed into the cushions. Nothing can prepare someone for how hard it is to wake up with arthritis in one's knees, or the shaking off a body that refuses to move when commanded.

That feeling is also true when a loved one passes, and after Mary died, I was going through a similar process. Her death had been something for which I had been preparing for years, and although the reality of it still surprised me, it was not something I felt was unexpected. She was sick, and that sickness had killed her. That much was simple to me. What was harder was trying to pretend my life would be the same without her. I kept reasoning that she had been dead for a long time before she actually died, that the meds had made her a different Mary from the person I knew. Only one part of that statement rang true though. Although Mary was not herself for the last 6 months of her life, she was not dead. I knew that, because I knew how I felt now that she *was* dead. No amount of prior expectation helped me cope with that, it would just be something that I would have to live with.

I found myself holed up in my room more than I ever had before, content with listening to the same 23 songs on my Walkman.

I remember my 12th birthday party in mid-September, almost 3 months after Mary's death. All of my friends had been invited to Taliano's. Janet had organized the whole thing, rushing to make sure we had enough invitations for the dozen kids that showed up and gift bags for them when they departed. We sat at two tables that had been pushed together to accommodate our big party. I sat in the middle—the birthday boy. I remember looking at Janet mid-way through the party, admiring her. "*It must have been hard to do all of this completely by herself*," I told myself. I looked back down at the crumbs on my plate, more full than I had realized. I gazed at my friends, who were all smiling.

It was weird, not because they were smiling—that was great. No, what was weird was that the birthday boy was not the center of attention at his own party. He sat in the middle of the table, but he kept failing to make elongated eye contact with his peers. He kept failing to engage them in conversation, and he kept looking down at his empty plate. This was his event, but no one entering the restaurant would have guessed it. The party seemed like an event for his friends to catch up with each other, rather than a celebration of his life at 12 years. He went home glad his friends had had a chance to interact with each other, but remained disappointed in himself for failing to be happy on his own day. His mind was full of complaints, reasons for his depression. *His friends all went to different schools than he did now. It was the first birthday without her. Everything was an excuse. Everything was a reason for him not be happy. He failed to realize that his friends were still there for him, that all he needed to do was reach out, instead of retreating into himself.*

Chapter 29: Life

Life had changed in other ways as well. Janet and I were now seeing a boring grief counselor, and I was in my eighth month on antidepressants, which I fought taking every day. I remember slipping them under my tongue and spitting them out constantly. I HATED the idea of relying on an external substance to "heal me." Mama was dead, and she was not coming back. The depression I felt from that could never be helped by any kind of pill claiming to cure a chemical imbalance in my brain. Taking a psychological medication at all was stupid to me. I felt as though taking antidepressants confirmed the fact that I NEEDED a substance to feel all right. I was a prideful individual who hated asking his math teacher for help for fear of being considered weak. I did not like the idea of turning to a pill to "cure me" of my ill when I thought I could do it myself.

I had the exact same feelings about being put on ADD medication. The psychologist proclaimed that I did not have the "hyperactive" element of the "disorder," but that I would do well to take the pills for my attention problems in class. She was not mistaken—the pills did help, as did the antidepressants she prescribed. I had to admit that I felt less hopeless with the antidepressants and more focused with the ADD meds. It is entirely possible that the drugs acted as placebos, and it is also entirely possible that the pills did their scientifically designated duties. Either way, I was more relaxed, more focused.

However, that still did not mean that I was comfortable with people knowing I took pills. I was concerned about taking ADD pills because I was worried that people would label me "slow," if they found out. The fact that I was taking a pill seemingly because I was inadequate in an intellectual area bothered me, and made me contemplate the very thought myself. *Why did*

I need a pill when others did not? I asked myself. *Why did I need a chemical to help me in math class? Was I stupid?* Part of me believed I was, and believed others would, too.

Still, what scared me most were the antidepressants. The moment the doctor told me I would be put on Wellbutrin, I thought about being 50 years old, having grey hair, and still taking my medication every day. It was a sobering thought, a nightmare of what I saw my life becoming. The problem was that I knew I needed the antidepressants. It took me a long time to admit, but it was true. I could go a week without feeling any significant symptoms, but then things would change. My appetite would increase and I would feel the need to keep eating right after lunch or dinner. In the afternoon I would feel a lethargy that was impossible to shake. The fatigue would carry into the night, making completing a simple writing assignment seem like the biggest hill in the world. The fatigue carried into the next day, and then the next, until it felt like I was simply going through the motions of life. As anyone with any form of depression understands, you have good days and bad days. The bad days can come out of nowhere, clawing at your insides. On those days you feel like you cannot do anything right, as if everything that is wrong with your life will stay that way forever. Attempts to climb out of your rut are more than difficult. Attempts not to cry are sometimes hard. On those days, suicide isn't contemplated. It is rather a sense of hopelessness, of apathy, of an overwhelming tiredness. It is paralyzing.

The longer I went without the pills, the more the fatigue enveloped me. I pushed on, on sheer will, convinced that I would be able to shake the depression off, that my pain was temporary. At some point though, I realized that my bad days, which were once a week-to-week occurrence, now happened every 3 to 4 days. It was realizing that I was crying in the front seat of Janet's car for reasons I could not quite ascertain. It was being afraid that my mom could see the apathy written on my face, the knowledge that with each passing day it was getting harder and harder to hide.

Even with all of that though, I still did not go back on the pills. Being sad and tired was better than being okay and medicated. Janet was the one who said enough.

"Ok—that's it," she said as I continued to sob into the car seat, "We're going to the hospital." I wanted to argue, but part of me was glad she had said something. I had been fighting the good fight for a long time. It felt good to imagine an end in sight. Three hours later, we were leaving the hospital with a written prescription in hand. I stared at it like it was a midterm marked with the letter "F." It might as well have been. The struggle I went through to fight taking the medication all felt useless. Now there was no point in fighting Janet every day when she set down my pill with a glass of OJ. Now there was no point in trying to hide my pill behind my tongue and spit it out later.

So I just sat there, staring at the bag with the prescription on it, wishing my depression would just evaporate, wishing all those people who had said happiness was all in your attitude were right.

A few hours later I sat in my bed, mulling a new challenge, and resolving to beat it. I knew it would be tough, and knew I needed all the help I could get. I glanced at the pill bottle by my dresser then dozed off.

Chapter 30: New

Going to a new school is not fun. You don't know anyone. You do not know where your classes are. You don't know which clique to appeal to, and... *you don't know anyone*. For me, that scenario was my seventh-grade experience. The school was called Parkmont and the days were called long. The kids were nice but they just didn't "get" me. They didn't understand that I didn't like Yugioh card games, or that a fun day for me consisted of a soccer ball and not a PlayStation. All these years I had begged to be normal and now I was—I was an unpopular seventh grader, the most normal thing a 12-year-old could be. That did not make it any easier, though, a fact I was reminded of every week. It grew tiresome enough that I faked sick on random days just to avoid going.

One of those days was a Tuesday in September. I really didn't feel like going to school and so I feigned great sickness to Janet, who took off work to care for a child that was perfectly healthy. It was sometime after seven in the morning, still early enough to go back to sleep. However, I did not feel like going back to sleep. Once I was up, I was up. I walked down to the kitchen and grabbed a peach yogurt from the fridge and poured myself a glass of orange juice as I did every morning. As the years passed, yogurt had actually started to taste good (go figure). I opened the top and brushed past our weary dog, running back to my room to relax and enjoy myself on my day off. The first order of business was turning on the TV and watching something entertaining. I hoped to find some reruns of *Saved By the Bell* or something. It was not on, and neither was the *Fresh Prince of Bel Air*. I scrolled some more—absolutely nothing was on, not even *Arthur*, the fun and self-aware children's cartoon. I gave up and turned to the news, figuring there would be something good after it. The local weatherman was doing his thing, a cheesy grin on his face. I groaned, ready to change the channel, when a news bulletin flashed across the bottom of the screen… something about a helicopter crash…. the reporters were saying that some newsman had been flying too low and had run into a building in New York. I hoped no one was hurt, although I suspected the low-flying news reporter was gravely injured. The NBC newsman suddenly corrected himself as he was told something in his ear… "We are now getting reports…we are now getting reports that a PLANE has flown into the World Trade Center," he said. "Here is the footage and as you can see the plane fly *directly* into the World Trade Center."

Suddenly there was another news flash at the bottom of the screen, *"A large scale fire has been reported in downtown DC."*

I thought of Janet. I couldn't remember if she had said whether or not she was going into work for a second to pick up some documents. Neither one of us had cell phones at the time and so I had no way of contacting her to make sure she was all right. Fortunately, my worries were all but forgotten moments later as a loud "thud" signaled her entrance into the household. I walked downstairs and filled her in on the morning's events. She had heard it already on the radio and reported to me that the "fire" downtown was the result of another 747 that had flown directly into the Pentagon. I went back upstairs and turned on the TV… EVERY single channel was covering both emerging stories. I remembered Janet telling me that the group responsible for this was currently unknown… though I remembered her later mentioning the names "Gaddafi" and "Bin Laden." Another header ran across the screen… "Second plane hits World Trade Center, confirmed as terrorist attack."

There it was right in front of my eyes… a white plane soaring through the clear blue sky with a clear destination… and then it crashed, cutting through the building like a knife. I couldn't believe what I was seeing was real. It really *was* like a movie... everybody was running for their lives as the news cameras zoomed down to Ground Zero. Huge ash clouds covered the streets and enveloped the people. Suits that were navy blue were now light grey. Faces that were pale were now tan... crews of CNN News' vans scrambled to the scene to get a good picture of what was happening on the ground in real time. I went downstairs to watch the unfolding events with Janet. Her face was as pale as those of the news reporters. I was fully aware that this event was a big deal, but seeing her face really brought it home. She understood so much more about U.S. history than anyone I would ever know... and if she was this shaken by this event... it was surely unprecedented. Her eyes, slightly sunken with the passing of time, began to tear. She did not say a word for several minutes. We just sat there, transfixed at what was unfolding.

An hour or so later I realized that I had fallen asleep... "Oh, my God" woke me up.

"Oh, my God," Janet proclaimed as the first tower fell, her palms covering her face. For what seemed like hours she remained silent, breaking it only when the second tower fell. "Holy shit," she said as the building fell to the earth. Tears streamed from her face as the orange and yellow flames lit up the early morning sky.

It was hard to watch, all those people who lost loved ones. At least in our case we had had time to prepare for the death of a loved one mentally; these people were not so lucky. I didn't know the full magnitude of the situation, but I knew I was supposed to show emotion, that this was not a normal calamity. I knew it was bad because the reporters did not know how to carry themselves. They had no witty quips or dire quotes to share. They seemed just as shocked as my mom was, unable to fill their airtime with words. Ten seconds, 15 seconds, 30 seconds would pass before they were able to find their next sentence.

"It looks like…" one newsman said vaguely, trailing off.

"It almost looks like a movie, doesn't it?" Another woman said grimly, finishing his sentence. Silence accompanied her statement as the viewers at home were bombarded with split screens of the victims, emergency personnel, and loved ones of those already lost. The same screens were shown on ESPN, Comedy Central, MTV, and Cartoon Network. It was as if America had stopped on its hinges—as if comedy, sports, and cartoons no longer existed.

Some events galvanize a town. Some galvanize a state. And some galvanize a country. September 11, 2001 was that event. The country did not respond as it did after Pearl Harbor. Women did not go to work in the steel mills while their husbands went off to battle. Men did not enlist in the army in record tallies. However, the togetherness that I felt from every stranger that week is how I imagine people in felt in 1941. The events had been horrible, but they had brought us together, if only for a few months. I remember walking and having people actually stop and talk to me as if I were in the most charming Southern town. I can't remember ever feeling as "one" with my fellow man as I did in the days following those four plane crashes. Everyone was so nice to one another, which was sad in a way. It took an event that large and that catastrophic for people to bond with one another.

The funny thing about life is that it always goes on. After a while people stopped talking to one another, doors were locked again, and people became suspicious of each other once more.

Chapter 31: Adolescent Misgivings

Meanwhile, life went on for me as well. I slogged through the maze that was adolescence. I got crushes on girls, lost crushes on girls, worried about my grades, and marveled at how my body continued not to change.

When I was not doing one of those things I was trying to connect with my new therapist. Her room, with its toy blocks, colorful carpet, and bouncy balls, was more equipped for someone 6 years my junior. Her tone matched the room, arching and playful, as if she was expecting a group of kindergarteners to interrupt her session. The questions she posed seemed the same session after session. I could only answer, "So how do you feel about that now?" so many times.

It did not take long for me to figure out that what I really wanted to figure out was how to cut our 60-minute sessions down to 30 minutes, and our 3-day-a-week meetings down to 1. Eventually I managed to surpass my goals, cutting the sessions down to zero. It was by far my greatest achievement in therapy. I saw that the sessions, while helpful at the beginning, had stalled. Throwing clay at the wall, and expressing how my day was to a friendly acquaintance were no longer enough to quell the angst I felt every day. It was not anybody's fault, but I knew it was time to move on. I told Janet, and within a couple weeks I was out of the colorful room for good.

However, I had not managed to escape the therapist's couch altogether. Indeed, the same week I left the grief counselor I was back for my 4:00 p.m. appointment with my psychiatrist, Dr. Hyden-Ester. She was the *pill lady*, as I thought of her in my mind. Right after my meltdown, one of Janet's friends had referred her to us, and now here we were.

Dr. Hyden-Ester was a tall, dark, and slender African-American woman with a welcoming voice and bright white teeth that looked as if they should have been in braces just a *little* longer. She directed Janet and I into the room and asked both of us to take a seat. She always opened by asking me to pick an emotion out of the dozens of faces on her wall. I always chose bored, tired, frustrated, or happy. I rarely felt the latter, but I felt like I was far enough from sad to make the leap sometimes. Dr. Hyden-Ester wore the same expression no matter what emotion I picked. "And why do you think you're feeling that way today?" She asked in a monotone yet nurturing voice.

"I don't know," I would say every session, a faraway look in my eyes. "I really don't. I'm just tired." I said.

"What was your day like today?" She would ask inquisitively.

"I don't know," I said. "The same I guess. It was normal. I, I just don't have any energy," I said. "It feels like I'm just going through the motions."

"Well, that's a common feeling for someone with depression to have," she said soothingly. "It does not mean there is anything wrong with you." I tried to fix my face into what I thought looked like a welcoming smirk, but what turned out to be a painful grimace. "Here's what we're going to do," she said calmly. "I am going to keep your dosage of Wellbutrin the same for now, and I want you to tell me how you're feeling on your next visit. I need to keep track of how much sleep you're getting at night and whether or not your appetite is fluctuating. If you still feel this way in a few weeks, then we'll try going to a higher dosage or try something new," she said.

"Okay," I said.

"Great," she said cheerfully. "Why don't you go out and get your mom—and we'll wrap this up so you can get home?" I nodded, careful not to move too fast even though Dr. Hyden-Ester had just hinted it was okay for me to want to leave.

I walked into the waiting room brusquely. "She said she'd like to see you now," I said.

"Okay," Janet said, setting down the book she had brought. We walked through a cramped hallway before pushing open the door leading back to Dr. Hyden-Ester's office.

"Have a seat," Dr. Hyden-Ester said warmly to Janet, beckoning her to take a seat on the couch. "So how is everything going?" she asked.

"It's going all right." Janet said, looking at me.

"Good," Dr. Hyden-Ester said. "I was just talking to Tony about some things we think might be of some good."

"Oh?" Janet said inquisitively.

"Yes," Dr. Hyden- Ester said. "Tony has been complaining of feeling tired, which is perfectly normal.

"However, what we were saying—and what I am thinking now, is that it would be good for Tony to chart how much sleep he is getting a night, as well as when he is having trouble sleeping. He's been through a lot these past couple of months—so have you," she said, gesturing to Janet. "I would be surprised if you both didn't feel a little tired. But when that fatigue keeps us from doing the things we're normally accustomed to doing, is when we begin to worry." (*AKA when we begin to add more pills, I thought.*) "From what Tony has told me, we aren't there yet," she said confidently. "However, if Tony is still feeling as tired and overwhelmed as he does now this time next month, we have discussed the possibility of increasing his current dosage." (*And... there it is, I thought.*) "Right now though, I would like to stay right where we are. I think overall, Tony is doing better than when he first came in, and you guys," she said, pointing towards Janet and me, "seem to be getting along better as well. Adolescence is a hard time anyway, I wouldn't want to complicate that by giving your brain more chemicals," she said, looking me in the eye.

It was a nice sentiment and all, but her message contradicted her proposed actions. If she was that focused on not altering my brain chemistry, she would not even have mentioned the possibility of increasing my dosage. *"Doctors always tell you what they think you want to hear,"* I thought. *"Regardless of what they're about to do."*

Dr. Hyden-Ester looked coyly at the clock, stood up, and shook both of our hands. "So I'll go ahead and write Tony a prescription for the three refills on the Wellbutrin," she said, ripping off a sheet of paper from her thick stack.

"Thanks," Janet said. "That should leave us set for a while."

"Great," Dr. Hyden-Ester said. "So—I guess I'll see ya next time then. Let me know if there are any problems; you can reach me anytime." She shook both of our hands briskly, opening the door for us.

"Thank you," I said.

"No problem," she said. "You guys have a safe trip back."

"Will do," Janet said, walking out of the door. We walked down the handicapped ramp leading to the car. I opened the door quickly, eager to get home as fast as possible. Janet started up the car and we were off once again. I spent the time sleeping.

***

It's funny. All of my experiences from a therapeutic perspective were the typical "white America" response to deep seated emotional issues. I was thrown pills and doctors like they were hot dogs at a baseball game. There was always a need to make sure I got the proper treatment for my "unnatural" condition. Mary died when I was 2 months away from my 12th birthday, and I was on antidepressants 8 months later. Janet asked me if I was open to taking the medication, and I grudgingly agreed. I was at my wit's end trying to figure out why it was so hard to be happy, and was ready and willing to try something new. Being told that my depression was due to a chemical imbalance in the brain, and not some deep-seated emotional weakness, was good to hear. And if my brain was imbalanced, I figured the drugs would cure me. But it was never that simple. The meds helped, but that was only half the battle. Part of being happy, comes from believing you can be (go figure). Pills can make it easier to adopt that mindset, but they cannot *make you happy.* I wish a little more emphasis were placed on that fact when I was in the doctor's office. Positive thinking alone was not enough to dissolve my issues; they were too concrete. However, thinking positively helped to chip away at those walls. I know, because today they look thinner and thinner. Some days are not my favorite, but I make it a point to take at least one positive thing from my experience. I believe in myself, and I believe I can build on yesterday. I still take Wellbutrin every day, but I am no longer ashamed to say it. My dosage has decreased from when I was 12, and I am generally a much happier person than I was then. I realize that the medicine is not a crutch, but a tool to help me be the best person possible.

From my side of the table, it seems as though children of minorities and children of the "typical" white family need to come to some happy medium when it comes to discussing whether or not to use medications to cure their ills. To millions of minority parents across the nation, medication is a topic broached when a child's cranium has been spilt open and not a second sooner. Medications for depression and ADHD are used sparingly in minority households in relation to the white majority population. The reason for this is that in most minority households there is no such thing as "depression" or "ADHD." Blacks, Latinos, and Asians in my experience, believe more in just "dealing" with depression. If someone is depressed, it is thought to be a temporary state of mind, or a result of a negative personality. "She's just a dark person." "He always finds something to whine about." "He's always been a crybaby," are sentences used to devalue an individual's underlying condition, which is often the product of a truly chemical imbalance. However, in these households, there is no such thing as having a chemical imbalance in the brain. You are the only one responsible for how you feel. If you feel depressed, it is your own fault. You can control how you react to things. You can control how happy you want to be. It becomes hard for the person with depression to explain that for them this is not the case. Those individuals fail to see that there are others like them, and that how they feel is not entirely their fault. Depression is sometimes genetic, just like any other illness. Just like alcoholism, or breast cancer, or Alzheimer's, certain individuals are more likely to be predisposed to it. Not every individual with depression knows this, but they should, because that lack of knowledge can result in the individual blaming him or herself for their condition.

That same lack of knowledge leads others to blame them as well. It is a cycle, one in which we blame the victim and cast the person who would consider taking their own life as "selfish." We fail to talk about the fact that the self-esteem of those in deep depression is so low that they may feel as though their loved ones lives would truly be easier without them, without the burden they believe they cause. Tossing pills to those who feel that way will not permanently reverse those thoughts. Pretending those thoughts aren't valid will not either. However, supporting that depressed person, teaching them that's it's okay to love themselves, supporting them if and when they decide to seek medical help for their condition, and fostering a loving community for them to exist in, might.

Unfortunately, depression is just one of many mental conditions written off from time to time within some households. For example, "He's just a li'l retarded" is an example of how members of many families react to particular relatives who would be labeled with autism in other households. Millions of high-functioning kids with autism are not simply "slow." They are not "stupid." Their brains are simply wired differently than the average kid's. Their capacity to understand is not the same as ours, but they can understand, and talk. We just have to listen better.

Kids with learning disabilities often face the same hardships. Math is not their thing. They fail it repeatedly. They have trouble grasping geometric concepts, naming shapes. They are not stupid either, they just learn differently, and need a different set of methods to help them along in their progression. However, to many, they are still simply "slow."

My grandmother liked to address me this way whenever she had the opportunity. The fact that I was on ADHD medication became proof that I was slow. "You know that boy a li'l slow," she liked to say when I struggled to find something in the house she had asked for. "You know that's why they send him to that small school," she said as my extended relatives stood there awkwardly, failing to offer any kind of support for a boy not yet brave enough to stand up for himself.

In the meantime, I continued to get lessons on why I needed to. Every time I struggled, my grandmother was sharp to point it out. At first I was angry, offended at constantly being labeled stupid. After a while though I started to believe she had a point. After all, I was on medication to help me focus. I did go to a small school that helped kids with learning disabilities, and I did seem to have trouble grasping simple directions quickly. Janet kept reassuring me that I was smart, but the "facts" seemed to lean in another direction. *Smart people didn't need to go to a school with small class sizes. Smart people didn't need extra time on their tests. Smart people didn't have visual/spacial learning disabilities.* Had Grandma never uttered a word to me, these thoughts would have been on my mind. When you believe you are not good enough, you do not need an affirmation from anyone else. It just becomes something that you take with you wherever you go. It is a thought process, a belief. When someone says something negative pertaining to that belief, it only reinforces the thought process.

Such was the case for me, and millions like me. I failed to be proud of myself—of the smart person I knew I was. I knew deep down that taking pills did not mean that I was not awesome. However, I let society trick me into thinking I was different from them. I let society tell me that cool kids didn't need to take pills. I let society make me feel inferior. I let it taunt me for being brave enough to admit I needed help. I let it bash me in front of others. My grandmother was a part of that society, but only a part. If she had not put me down, someone else would have. That's what society does to us. It makes us think it is okay to make fun of people for being different. It capitalizes on our need to fit in. When we feel we do not, it throws us medicine that is supposed to help us blend better. It confuses us. It tells us that it is okay to be different if we are prettier, richer, smarter, or taller. But that it is not okay to be different if we are ugly, handicapped, or poor. My grandmother was just a product of that society. That same society told her being a woman was not okay. That same society told her being black was not okay. She was just trying to fit in, too.

Society does something else to us though: it throws us curveballs. Whenever we think we have it all figured out, it throws a new wrinkle into the mix. My grandmother would soon be reminded of that fact.

Chapter 32: Thanksgiving

Thanksgiving was different in 2011, and by different I mean good. Almost all of my cousins were there, and my grandmother seemed to be in good spirits. Her face was contorted in a smile rather than a frown. Her eyes twinkled rather than glared.

"How are you doing in college?" She asked as I walked up to the table.

"I'm doing all right." I said "just working hard."

"That's good, babeh," she said in that raspy voice of hers, setting an unlit cigarette down on an old astray.

"So what are your post-college plans?" one aunt chimed in. "After graduation I plan to go to law school," I said meekly. "Get outta town!" she exclaimed.

"Seerita's doing that now. So when are you taking the, the…"

"LSAT," I interrupted.

"Yeah, the LSAT, I can't keep track of all of those tests."

"I understand," I said. "I can hardly keep track of them myself."

"Yeah, well, you should talk to Seerita because she's been taking some classes for that," she said. I contorted my body awkwardly, trying to locate Seerita's face from the dozen or so in the room.

"Hey, Seerita!" someone called. "Tony said he's taking that law school test soon."

"Send him over!" I heard Seerita shout.

I was herded over to the couch, where I took my seat beside her.

"Here," she said, passing me a note.

"This is the name of the teacher I'm taking my LSAT class with. He is a really good teacher and the class is legit."

"Thanks, Seerita. I'll definitely check it out." I said.

Seerita looked me in the eye, smirking "No prob, cuz," she said—"I got your back." "So," she said abruptly, changing the subject. "I know an AKA who's about your age, you want me to hook you up?"

"If you want to you can... but I'm doing fine on that front," I said confidently.

My grandmother, who was listening more intently than I thought, strolled up next to me.

"You got a girlfriend?" she said.

"No," I replied.

"And you how old?"

"21."

...   "You got a boyfriend?" She said brazenly.

"No I do not—I'm not gay." I said, smiling for effect.

Bouts of laughter were heard from my aunts, a couple of chuckles from my cousins, and a smirk from my grandmother, who shuffled away. It was the first time I told her flat out that I was not gay, as opposed to saying; "I like women," or "No, I do not have a boyfriend." She seemed to take it well enough. Part of me even thought I had impressed her.

I turned back to the couch, reliving the minor breakthrough. "Who's that?" Seerita asked, interrupting my moment. I turned my head, searching for the body Seerita mentioned. I craned my neck, spotting a dark-skinned woman with black high heels, skinny blue jeans, and a small white coat that clung to her body. As the woman strutted up to my grandmother several thoughts crossed my mind:

Why is she walking in here dressed like that? So much of her lower back is showing that I wouldn't be surprised if her ass crack skipped out and played four square with everyone.

Also...That long black curly weave is mighty ostentatious for a Thanksgiving meal.

Suddenly I remembered that Seerita had actually asked me a question.

"I have no idea who that is," I said.

"Is that... is that...Mi-kel?" She asked.

"Umm... yeah, I guess it is."

I was stunned. There stood my cousin Mi-kel, black curly weave and all. Dolled up like an easy girl on 14th street. The same boy I had grown up with. The same child I had seen so many times in my childhood visits. The same kid who once said "Why is Tony here? He's not in the family."

Now here he was standing five paces away from me—in drag. He wore no makeup apart from his black eyeliner. His toothy grin was the same as ever. The hug he gave my grandmother was heartfelt.

And all this time I thought this family disliked gay people, and here they are proving me wrong. I thought. *Here they are hugging and showing affection to Mi-Kel.* I felt a rush of anger and relief. Anger because they didn't accept *my* family, and relief because maybe they never cared either way about my mom's being gay... maybe they were just heartbroken that I chose another family over theirs.

I stared at Mi-Kel as he walked back to the porch to get something. I settled in my seat, putting the scene out of mind for a second. By this time it was around 4:00 p.m. and my belly was getting angry with me. Introspection could wait.

Not a second later, Mi-Kel came bursting through the kitchen, yelling incoherently. My Uncle Greg followed him, his face screwed up in blind furry. "What did you say?!" He yelled.

"WHAT DID YOU SAY?!" Greg kept shouting as he followed Mi-Kel out of the front door, past the sidewalk, and into the street. I, along with half a dozen others, rushed to the door to see what the commotion was about.

"YOU DON"T KNOW ME!" Mi-Kel was shouting in his high heels and high-pitched voice.

BOY, I'LL FUCK YOU UP!" Greg was shouting now.

"MMM HMM, GO 'HEAD! GO 'HEAD! YOU DON"T EVEN KNOW WHAT YOU DOING. I'LL COME TO YOUR HOUSE AND BOMB IT… I'LL BOMB THE WHOLE THING!" Mi-kel said.

"**WHAT!?**" Greg shouted.

"GREG HAS SOMETHING IN HIS HAND! GREG HAS SOMETHING IN HIS HAND!" People were shouting.

"FUCKING FAGGOT!" Greg shouted, pointing a shaky index finger at Mi-Kel.

"YOU DON"T KNOW ME!" Mi-kel said. "YOU BETTER WATCH YOUR BACK! "

Greg moved closer and closer to Mi-Kel as the screams grew louder.

"GREG HAS SOMETHING IN HIS POCKET!"

Greg is a police officer, and I am fairly certain that he did in fact have something in his pocket. Luckily for all of those involved, this something was never seen. Greg was talked down by several of my uncles, and walked back inside. Mi-Kel kept shouting as he got into a friend's car and drove off.

Greg entered the house in a huff. "Y'ALL KEEP PUTTING UP WITH THAT SHIT!

"SHIT!" He said angrily.

After some prodding from his wife Greg calmed down, although he did call the cops and felt he had cause to do so, given the fact that Mi-Kel had threatened to bomb his house.

I looked over to my grandmother for a reaction. What I saw was completely different than what I would have imagined. Her face sunk as she started to sob quietly, her toothless mouth open for everyone to see, tears running down her cheeks.

"I knew this day was going too well," she said.

I felt like I was watching something indecent, turning away.

The whole situation was surreal. I remember having the distinct urge to laugh. This urge often comes over me in extremely awkward moments; I believe that it is my body's defense mechanism to the unknown. My Aunt Robin, who may have the same defense mechanism, turned her gaze from Greg towards me.

"You haven't seen anything like that before have you, Tony? That's a good old fashioned African-American family episode," she said proudly.

She turned and opened her arms as if proclaiming to a wide audience.

"Tony became African-American today."

All I could do was smile. It was not the first time she had publicly addressed my blackness, and it would not be the last. It was just something being raised by white people brought me. I had accepted long ago that there would be those in the family who would deem me not only less black, but not black at all, because of who raised me. It was okay. That was their opinion, and I honestly had to admit that if I had not done much to change it. I still used little slang, showed no interest in joining a historically black fraternity, never brought any friends with me, black or white, and never had a black girlfriend with me to show off. It did not matter that I knew more black history than most my age, or that I considered it my duty to represent myself in a way that would make the black men and women who fought for human rights proud. It did not matter because they did not know any of that, and I had never rectified that.

Instead, I had stopped caring what they thought, which had probably confirmed what they had expected—that I simply did not care about black culture. It took me a long time to learn that the only way to show them I cared was by coming out of my shell and interacting with them more. To understand that a strong black man could be raised in a white-headed household, they needed to meet that man.

Soon they would, but today was not that day. No, today represented something different entirely. A seismic shift had occurred, one I could not have foreseen in the previous years. My grandmother—the soldier, the pit-bull, was changing right before my eyes. Mi-Kel's entrance would have normally elicited at least a harsh barb. The fact that he remained unscathed was nothing short of a miracle. Mi-Kel had come out of the closet—in extraordinary fashion. Whether or not my grandmother knew Mi-Kel was gay before that day is unclear. The fact that she took it upon herself to hug him upon his entrance, though, showed me that she still wanted him to be a part of the family. And although it surprised me that Grandma of all people had softened her stance, or at least failed to mention it—that was the first sign that something was wrong. The fact that she broke down after Mi-Kel left, rather than admonishing him or Greg for their behavior, was out of character as well. The woman who yelled at me when I chose Mary and Janet over her family was nowhere to be found. The woman who told my sister she was getting fat or that I needed to eat less pizza when she saw a pimple on my face had disappeared from view. She was replaced by this "Grandma," this soft woman who was a pleasant person to be around. I walked away from her house that day knowing she had changed. The bigger question was why.

Chapter 33: The Second

It was one o'clock on a hot September day. I sat in my cramped and cluttered cubicle surfing for new music to zone out. I was halfway across the world in my mind, out in the ocean in Hawaii somewhere, when the top of my phone started blinking, alerting me of a new message. I reluctantly reached across the brown desk, opening my battle worn BlackBerry to reveal the text. I scrolled down the screen, opening a message that was marked "Angela." I pressed another button, revealing the entire message. "Grandma in ICU," it said. "Are you in DC or Baltimore?"

"I'm in Balt, but I'll come back now to visit Grandma." I replied without hesitation to my sister.

I put down the phone, weighing my emotions. I twiddled my thumbs for a couple of seconds, contemplating my next move. I stood up, brusquely walking out of the room into the hallway. I took a few paces then turned the corner, walking up to my supervisor's office. I knocked politely on a half-open door, then spoke without waiting to be spoken to: "Hey, I just wanted to let you know that I have to leave early today; my grandmother is in the hospital."

"No problem," Joanne said in a nurturing voice. "Take as much time as you need." I nodded in approval and before I knew it, I was sitting in my car on I-95, driving home as fast as I could. Angela's message had been fairly vague, and if I missed seeing my grandmother today I feared that I would not get another chance. I met Janet at home and from there we drove in her blue car to Washington Adventist Hospital. The car ride brought back memories. I reminisced about all the afternoons Janet and I had driven to see Mary in the cancer ward at the same hospital. Suddenly I was warped into a past life I thought I had left behind. "I'll wait for you here," Janet said, snapping me out of my reverie. I heard myself say "okay" before absentmindedly swiping a visitor's pass from a friendly face at the front counter. I walked to the elevator nonchalantly, exuding a false calm. After waiting a few moments for the doors to open, I shuffled in and pressed the white, oval button, marked with a black "3" and waited patiently as the elevator moved slowly up floors one and two. After what seemed like an eternity, the elevator door came to a halt. I stepped out as the gray doors slid open, confused about where I was. I walked down a long corridor, searching for someone to guide me. After a short while, I was greeted by the sincere face of an older doctor who looked beaten down by the day's events.

"Do you know where I can find the ICU?" I asked.

"Yes, you're on the right floor but you're in the wrong wing," he said. "The ICU is on the other side."

"Thanks." I said. "I'll head that way then."
He nodded and returned to whatever grim events lay waiting for him a few feet away.

I spent the next few minutes wandering the halls, trying not to get lost again. I failed in that attempt, but eventually found where I needed to be. Just down the hall read a sign labeled "Intensive Care Unit." My shoes squeaked as I hustled down the blue floor, unsure of what awaited me. I approached silver doors with trepidation, steadying myself as they flew open with no warning. Three adult figures with tears on their faces shuffled out in agony, oblivious to my existence. I felt as if were invading their privacy by even being there. I turned away, looking across the hall to find a family of four sitting on a cold metal bench, sobbing silently into each others' arms.

I quickly turned my gaze back to the now open ICU door and strolled in, looking for the bed that held my grandmother.

"Excuse me." I said to the young, curly haired nurse by the front desk. "Can you tell me where Mary L. Davis's room is?"

She paused before glancing down at her chart.

"She's in room 102, to your left and in the corner. She may be asleep," she said.

"Thanks, I won't disturb her if that's the case," I said. I smiled curtly then walked down the hall, spotting her room.

The door was open and the place was dark, allowing a thin yellow film of sunlight to steal into the space and attach itself to her bedside. Her body was still, lifeless under the blue blanket. An IV line sat on the floor and snaked it's way under the covers, creating a soft imprint around a frail wrist. I looked down at my grandmother. Her face was gaunt and her lips were chapped and bleeding. Tubes resided in her mouth and nose, assisting her breathing but making it impossible for her to speak. Her thin gray hair was a mess, strewn over the pillow in different directions. I approached her slowly, unaware if she recognized me.

"Grandma?" I said.

"Grandma? It's me, Tony. Do you recognize me?"

She nodded.

"I'm here, Grandma. I'm here."

"Don't try to speak." I said as she struggled to maneuver her mouth around the tubes. "Do you want anything?" I said.

She shifted her eyes left to a shelf containing a water cooler.

"Okay. Okay. Hold on." I walked to the cooler and poured a small glass, carefully bringing the cup to her bedside.

Grandma opened her mouth as I held the glass steadily and poured the water gently down her throat. More water ended up on her hospital gown than in her mouth, but she seemed more relaxed all the same. Her lips returned to their natural color as drool escaped out of the side of her mouth. I wiped it off and sat down in the chair next to her.

"I got you this." I said. Pulling out a set of earrings I had bought the previous day. "See, I told you I'd get your earrings eventually," managing a nervous laugh. I took the earrings out of the box, holding them up for display. Grandma's eyes opened more than they had before, carefully examining her present.

"I know you can't wear them right now, but I'll leave them here for when you get out." I said, putting the blue earrings clumsily back in their box.

Grandma started to speak, uttering a raspy sequence of phrases.

"What?" I said. "Are you uncomfortable here?"

She nodded.

"Well, I can imagine why," I said shortly, glancing at the leftover JELL-O and turkey on the small plastic plate by her bedside.

"This food isn't nearly as good as yours." I said with a chuckle.

She smiled then shook her head.

The curly haired nurse walked in, carefully adjusting Grandma's pillows before leaving.

Grandma's face grew hard.

"Is it them? Is it the nurses? The doctors?" I said.

She nodded.

"Okay. Okay."

"Home," she mouthed.

"Home," she mouthed again.

"You want to go home?" I asked in a fragile voice.

She nodded again.

"Okay, Grandma. Okay. I'll let Aunt Robin know. I'll get you out of here. Okay?"

She nodded once more. I grasped her hand.

"I just want to say that I love you," I said calmly. "I know that you took care of a lot kids in the family when their parents couldn't take care of them." I said.

She nodded slowly.

"Thank you for doing that, and for keeping the family together." I said.

I bent down and kissed her on the forehead.

"I have to go now, Grandma, but I'll be back," I said. "I love you," I repeated.

She glanced up, taking me in one last time. She did not speak, but her lips softened and her eyes glistened, making her message clear.

I took her hand in mine, letting go after a few moments of silence, before walking out of the room.

I moved as if on auto pilot past the ICU's grey doors back toward the elevator, unaware that I had even pressed the down button when the doors slid open again. I stepped in and contemplated what to say to Janet, drawing little inspiration before the doors slid open once more two floors later.

I walked out of the elevator, past the soda machine, and past the waiting desk before spotting Janet in the corner, engrossed in her *Newsweek* magazine.

"Okay." I said abruptly.

"Ready?" She said hazily.

"Yea," I muttered.

"Let's go."

And with that, Janet stood up, marking her page with an old receipt and closing the magazine. We walked out and drove home, both of us contemplating what to say.
Janet broke the ice first.

"So... did the doctor's say what's wrong with her?"

"The doctor said she has pneumonia brought about by a weakened lung capacity brought about by a cancerous tumor." I said.

"Oh," Janet said.

"Well is she comfortable...?" She asked sweetly.

"No," I said. "She said she wants to go home."

"Well, who is responsible for her right now?" Janet said.

"Aunt Robin is."

"I think she'll be more comfortable at home, but it may be too hard to care for her there..." I said, trailing off.

Janet glanced at me then returned her eyes to the road.

We spent the rest of the car ride in silence, the sound of the tires rubbing against the gravel in our driveway the only thing to break it.

I walked in the house and got ready for bed, preparing myself for a week that figured to be a tough one.

I awoke the next morning feeling as though I hadn't slept at all, the image of Grandma's tired face still in my mind. I knew she wasn't doing well, and surmised that it was only a matter of time before more bad news arrived. Three days later, I received it.

"Grandma's going to be taken off of life support, the family is meeting at the hospital at 1

o'clock tomorrow." Angela's message read.

I was unable to put two and two together right away. Part of me felt as though this could

mean that the doctors had agreed to give Grandma a fighting chance to survive off of life

support to see if her condition improved, a practice I had heard of being used before.

It wasn't until I arrived at the hospital the next day that I understood. I walked through

the sliding doors with more than a little trepidation. Everything looked the same: the sign in

front of the marble welcome desk still read "Welcome," the vending machine held the same

lone Payday bar as before, the halls still smelled of stale bread, and the ICU waiting room was

still filled with old, burgundy chairs. The only difference was that today, every single one of the

chairs was filled. Almost everyone from the family was here. Everyone's heads were down, no

one spoke. Aunt Robin was the first to notice my presence, slowly getting up and slowly

moving across the room to greet me.

"Hey, Tony, thanks for coming." She said in a cracked but determined voice.

"No problem," I said shortly.

"Angie and the kids are here, too," she said. "They're all with Grandma, you can go in

and visit her too if you'd like."

"Thanks," I said. "I'd like that."

I hugged her before walking down the hall, maneuvering around two doctors before

reaching the room I was looking for. The door was open, the light still off. Angela stood by her

bedside, crying as she gently gripped Grandma's shoulder. Angela's daughter Courtney stood

next to her, holding her mother's hand. I walked up to my sister, hugging her as wet sniffles stuck to my chest. I grabbed a couple of tissues from the desk and handed them to her, placing the soft cotton in her palm.

"Thank you," she said, quietly dabbing her nose and eyes.

"No problem," I said, taking in everyone in the room for the first time. In the corner sat Grandma's daughter, Carolyn, and her son Greg. Her granddaughter, Seerita, was seated by her bedside while her granddaughter, Bonita, sat at the foot of her bed. The only sounds came from the sniffles of those surrounding the bed and the hum of the life support machine by the window.

I looked at my grandmother, examining all that I could. Her hair was more of a mess than it had been on my past visit, but she seemed more peaceful than she had been before, her chest heaving lightly up and down as she slept. Her face looked like that of someone about to die, gaunt, cracked—old. My cousin Bonita turned to Seerita and mumbled something in her ear.

"Everybody out y'all, let's give Bonita some time alone with Grandma," Seerita said.

I left the room first, heading to the bathroom before returning to the waiting room.

I found one of the ugly burgundy chairs and sat down next to my cousin Javon, who sobbed violently, holding both palms to her face. A woman to her right placed a timid arm around her, crying as well. My shoulders sagged, my eyes gazing at the floor. Aunt Robin walked into the room, her shoulders slumped as she walked up to my aunts and uncles.

"They taking her off life support now," she said quietly.

"How long does she have?" asked Aunt Kim.

"They don't know," Aunt Robin said.

"They said once in a while it takes a couple of days, but most of the time it takes an hour or two."

One aunt started to cry, another looked away. My Uncle Kevin sat in the corner, a withdrawn look on his face.

"They said it's okay for us to go in to see her," Aunt Robin said, sitting down.

Several people left the room immediately, shuffling down the hall. I stayed in my seat, still trying to take everything in. I looked to my right, putting my arm around Javon, who continued to sob passionately. A small woman to her right hugged her as I pulled my shoulder away, averting my gaze to the floor.

I stood up, briefly glancing at the forlorn faces surrounding me before setting off to Grandma's room.

My shoes squeaked against the hard, linoleum floor as I made my way to her door. I peeked in. Angela stood by her bedside in the same spot as before, crying openly. Bonita sat in the corner, tears running down her cheeks. My uncle Greg sat by Grandma's bedside clasping her hand, holding back tears.

I turned to Grandma, whose pupils dilated as she struggled for breath, grasping for air that was no longer there. Suddenly she began to convulse, her shoulders shaking as drool dripped from the sides of her mouth, coating the bed in liquid. Her neck tightened as her chest heaved back and forth, unable to relax itself as it had only minutes before. Her face contorted in such a way that made it possible to see each and every line of her cheek as it ballooned and then sunk. The bed shook as her back shook against the mattress, sending the surrounding pillows to the floor. Her nostrils flared as she tried to find her breath, choking violently.

Uncle Greg turned from Grandma.

"Get the children out!" He said, his voice breaking.

"Get the children out!" He said, even more forcefully than before. "They don't need to see this!"

He faced the rest of the room.

"Grandma wouldn't want y'all to see her like this," he said, tears running down his cheeks.

"Go on now… go on," he said, trembling.

I turned to my sister, holding her hand. She turned to me, looking me in the eye, her cheeks now soaking wet.

"Why, Jesus, why!" My Aunt Carolyn shrieked.

"C'mon y'all, get out!" Uncle Greg said once more as we began to file out, leaving only Grandma's children in the room.

I looked back at his sullen face. In that moment he transformed from a responsible, professional parent to a child simply mourning the loss of his mother. The tears that streaked his cheeks made him look 30 years younger under the hollow glow of the afternoon sunlight, a reminder that on this day, he was just a kid, too.

People like to use the term "fade away," or "went peacefully," or "didn't suffer," when describing how someone dies. It makes people feel better to know their loved ones are going to a better place and that they didn't suffer or feel pain in their last few moments on earth. I wish that in every case this was so, but unfortunately, it is not. Death is harsh and cruel, a painful reminder that one day we may all have to suffer one final battle before departing for good.

For my grandmother, that battle raged on as she lay there dying. Thirty minutes later I sat in the waiting room, both hands on my knees.

Aunt Robin slowly came into the room, dragging her feet to the center of the floor. She hesitated before speaking.

"She's gone," she said, her voice a whisper as she removed her glasses to dab her eyes with a crumpled tissue.

"She's gone," she repeated, tears now gushing faster than a single tissue could hold.

Shrieks erupted around me, echoing off of the wall and into the hollow hallway. I looked up like a soldier in battle, trying to find the closest person to attend to. I spotted Angela, who sobbed into her hands, her arms hugging her knees.

"It's not fair!" She said violently. "I-I-I-I nev-er got to repair my relationship with her; now I never will! She probably didn't even love me," she said, trailing off.

"But she did love you," I said, walking over to her.

Angela interjected. "No, she didn't," she said quietly. I never got treated the same as the rest of the family, rarely got presents when they did… Grandma didn't love me."

"She did, she did," I said forcefully as Angela shook her head. I got down on my knees and looked her in the eye. "She did, Angie," I said, grabbing her hand. "I know because she told me last week. She said she loved both of us, Angie, and that she was proud of us. I told her that we were going to stay in contact and she smiled."

Angela took a deep breath. "She said that?" She uttered quietly.

"Yes."

"I just wish we had had a closer relationship. Now I'll never get the chance to talk to her to fix things."

"Yes, you will," I said. "Grandma will always be with you. She's right here," I said, pointing at her chest. "She's always there, whenever you want to talk, she's right there."

She looked up, nodding before returning her gaze back to the floor, teardrops falling on her grey Jordan sneakers. I softly slid my hand from hers before walking into the hallway, a blank expression on my face. I looked around at the surreal scene, taking it all in. I slouched against a cold wall, unable to compose myself, my eyes dropping to the floor. Grandma's son Clayton, who was crying himself, came up to me.

"Hey, man," he said wearily. "You okay?"

I hesitated before speaking. "Yeah, I'm okay," I said foolishly.

"I know man, I'm hurtin', too. Come here," he said, wrapping both arms around me. We hugged for a few seconds before separating. Both of us said a few kind words, and then went our separate ways.

I decided it was time to leave, grabbing my grey sweater from a nearby coat rack. I put it on and turned to leave before spotting Angie. I wandered over to my big sister, giving her one last hug before I left.

"I love you," she said while embracing me.

"I love you, too," I said.

"We're staying in town for the next couple of days. Let me know if you want to get together for lunch so we can celebrate your birthday."

"That sounds great," I said. "I'm free Friday."

"Great," she said. "You live in Takoma Park, right?"

"Yeah, we can meet up in Silver Spring, though."

"Great, I'll text you later. Goodbye, little brother," she said.

"Goodbye, Angie," I said, walking towards the elevator.

I pressed the black button marked "L" and waited patiently for the sliding doors to open, in no rush to do much of anything. Two floors later I was back at ground level, a weary expression on my face. I wondered through two sliding doors and stepped out into the sunlight, hopping into my car. I checked my cell phone. About an hour remained before class started, more than enough time to make it, barring traffic. I took a deep breath and turned on my radio, changing the setting to "auxiliary" so I could listen to tunes from my cell phone. I pressed play and selected the song "Creepers." There was something about the mellow melodic riffs and whining vocals that spoke to me. I spent the entire 45-minute ride playing that one song, reflecting on Grandma's death.

I thought her passing would be complicated to handle. She had been mean for so long, that I am ashamed to admit that there were times when. I hoped her death happened sooner rather than later. She had been old for so long that she seemed immortal. With her in the picture, I was obligated to interact with her and her family against my wishes, simply because the courts had deemed it appropriate. When the court lifted its order, I still felt a moral obligation to visit because deep down, I felt I owed it to her. Despite her abrasiveness, her harsh words, and her general decorum, she was still the one person who offered to raise me when I was born. Before and after I was adopted, she was not obligated to have me over for visits, or take care of me overnight, but did so, anyway.

It was for those reasons that I knew she loved me, and why losing her was much harder than I had anticipated. To know that someone who loved you unconditionally is dead is hard. When that someone is part of your routine, it is especially hard. Once they die, the routine may contain the same elements, but it never feels the same. In my case, those routines were holidays.

Every holiday I drove over the Anacostia River to see my grandmother. Every holiday we gathered around at her table to say grace. Now that she was gone, the routine would never be the same.

I thought that I would enjoy the end of the routine. I thought that I would enjoy not driving over those 18th-century roads to get to her house. I thought that I would enjoy my clothes not smelling like smoke every Thanksgiving. I thought that I would enjoy not having to listen to her accuse me of being gay. I thought I would enjoy not having to see her anymore.

I didn't enjoy anything about that car ride though, and I didn't enjoy seeing her in that hospital bed. Above all though, I didn't enjoy the fact that I would never get to see her again, if only to tell her that I loved her unconditionally, too.

Chapter 34: Gay Rights

The weeks following Grandma's death were completely different than the weeks following Mary's. There were no phone calls to the house, no flowers sent to our doorstep, and no kind letters waiting in the mailbox. I shed no tears, and talked little about how I felt to Janet or anyone else. My sorrow didn't compare to that of other members of the family, whose Facebook posts lit up my computer. Most members of the family saw Grandma far more often than I had. They were present at BBQ's, dinners, and celebrations that I never made it to. Many of them had also never experienced the death of a loved one before, an ordeal impossible to prepare for. For some, it may have been hard to grasp that Grandma had in fact lived the fullest life possible. She was 80 years young when she died, an admirable age for anyone, but astonishing, given her insatiable smoking habit. Indeed, she got away with doing what she wanted, when she wanted, for as long as she could, consequences be damned. In medical terms she died of pneumonia brought about by a complicated lung-related illness, but in layman's terms she died of old age, a condition we should all be so lucky to succumb to.

My present condition revolved around the sorrow I felt for my cousins, uncles, nieces, and aunts who knew my grandmother better than I. I felt for my Aunt Robin in particular, who was no longer working full time at NIH because Grandma had needed someone to look after her. Her mother was gone, as was a major portion of her life. She joked during the funeral that going over to Grandma's all the time was the secret to her and her husband's success.

"Now we'll actually have to talk to each other!" She said. Everyone laughed, knowing that Robin was only half joking. Grandma was a big part of her and her husband's life, and though I doubted their marriage would suffer, I understood my aunt's cause for concern. When someone close to you dies, everything in life seems less certain. People that were your rock and your purpose are gone, creating a scenario in which you wonder how long it will be before your other blessings will soon be distant memories as well.

Grandma's death forced me to look at my own blessings. Janet was one. She had stood by me, been a single mother to me after Mary died. She drove me to countless 9:00 a.m. soccer games 30 miles away—had replaced dozens of lost soccer socks. She dedicated herself to helping me with my math homework almost every night, even after a long workday.

I thought about how fortunate I was to have been adopted. I thought about my grandmother, about how different the world was when she fought that adoption 20 years prior.

During that time a significant portion of Americans would have sided with her argument. It was not as if she was putting forth a foreign idea. She believed, as many believed, that the best home for a child was one with a mother and father, but that in the absence of that, a home headed by two gay people was the last option that should be considered. I do not know how many people still believe this (I imagine many do). The difference is that today, they know it would be unwise to come out and say it.

We live in a peculiar society. One in which every president in our history has been Christian while there remains a separation of church and state. One in which the Lord's Prayer is recited at schools while Bible verses are not allowed to be taught. We live in a society in which our current president had to convince the nation he was a Christian, and not a Muslim, to avoid losing an election. We live in a society that saw his opponent convince the country that being a Mormon should not keep him from being elected, and that his faith shared the same Christian values as the nation's founders.

We also live in a society that is changing, and a society that preaches tolerance while some admonish those who speak their minds, if those thoughts are in violation of the status quo. Somehow, in a nation that in time came to define itself as a majority Christian one, we have gotten to the point where one of the most quoted lines in the Bible—the one that says "and for a man lie with another man—it is an abomination"—is no longer a valid argument against allowing a man and a man to marry. The separation of church and state has always been present, but it is obvious that in the case of homosexual marriage, church and state mixed together to make law. For years and years it was said that it was morally wrong for two gay people to get married. Not only because they were gay, but because they would conceivably want to start a family. Opponents argued that if they wanted to be gay that was one thing, but allowing innocent children to witness such a wrong, such an abomination, was too much.

Then everything started to change. There had been this movement; this *Gay Rights Movement*, that began to engulf the nation. Gays were now demanding equal treatment. They demanded that they too should have the same rights as every family. It was hard to imagine, *how could such an immoral action and lifestyle gain a reward that only legitimate families should have?* It was a weird sentiment. But now the entire country seemed to be embracing it. State by state they went. First New Hampshire, then California, then Maine—each legalizing the right of two men and two women to marry. Now men and women would be allowed to marry with no restrictions. Now they would be granted access to the same benefits as heterosexual married couples, *real* married couples. It was an affront to the values of the Bible, but it was more than that. These individuals, while well meaning, were trying to change the definition of what it meant to be a family, to raise a child. They may have been good people, but they were sinners. It was not a fact that was up for debate. And now, for some reason that was okay. It was okay for gay couples to start a family, to bring a child into the world.

The fabric of society was changing indeed. And on top of that, people who disagreed with it were being cast out, censured, forced to apologize. It was no longer okay for you to say you disagreed with the sinners. It was no longer okay to stand up for what you believed in as a good Christian. The politicians who you agreed with, who took a stand, were suddenly the bad guys. They were suddenly the ones who needed to change. Everyone was on this crusade, this drive to be politically correct. But it all happened too fast. The change happened too fast. Those who still believed in old-fashioned Christian values were still high in number and were still willing to stand up for the causes they believed in. The numbers of those within the counterculture were reflected across gubernatorial and senatorial races, where most of their candidates either won or came close to winning. The media may have acted as though the nation was now free to be gay. But they knew better. They understood that there were plenty of people just like them who wanted to see the nation get back to its Christian roots just as badly, and were just as fed up with the way things were going. However, they also understood that standing up for what they believed in could get them in a lot more trouble than it was worth. Therefore, it was better to remain silent, to put their chips in the politicians willing to fight the good fight.

If they needed to talk about their true feelings, the place to do it was with their friends and like-minded peers. It was not ideal, but it was better than walking around like nothing had changed. Women's groups, men's groups, Christian groups, college dorm rooms, smoke breaks, call-in radio shows, all became places for them to let off steam, to join up with the counterculture.

One day in November I stumbled into them. They were not happy to see me. I represented what was wrong with America, what they needed to change. I was not aware of what I had gotten myself into until it was too late.

***

It all started on a humid September day. I sat outside in a white chair under a fancy white pavilion. An attractive co-ed sat to my right, taking in the day's events. I glanced at her then followed her eyes to the stage where a middle-aged man with a booming voice addressed a tired crowd. "And thank you!" He said after ten inspired minutes, clearly running over his time allotment. The crowd clapped as he stepped away from the stage, making way for the headliner. The governor strode onto the stage with the confidence only a politician could muster—arrogant but warm. He smiled at the crowd before adjusting the mic to his taller height, than began his speech. "And we must put emphasis on education not just for the sciences, but for the arts as well," he said. "Your school president knows this, and is doing right by the school and by the educational institution in general by building this state of the art performing arts theater. It is with pleasure that I cut the ribbon today on this groundbreaking ceremony." Someone handed him a hard hat as he stepped away from the platform and closer to a big red ribbon by the bottom of the stage. He walked off the stage calmly, hard hat in hand, on his way to his destination. The crowd was silent as he took his last few steps up to the ribbon. He inhaled, and then cut the ribbon in half with a giant pair of scissors a young person had passed to him. He smiled broadly as the crowd clapped mildly, slipping on his hard hat. He looked pretty ridiculous. A man in a $2,000 suit wearing a hard hat—but I guess that was the point. "Who's gotta shovel?" He said confidently, looking for someone to hand him one. "Thanks," he said as our school president handed him a shiny one. "All right, let's do this!" He said, smiling again to the crowd. He and our university president knelt down, gripping two brand-new-looking shovels. They glanced at each other briefly, then at the crowd, before sinking the shovels deep into the earth. Applause erupted as the shovels clanked against rock, dirt, and grass. Both men looked at the crowd with satisfied looks on their faces, waving to the throng as if they had just won an election. "Thank you all for coming!" Our president said. "We have taken a huge step forward today, and will continue to work to make sure that work continues in the future. "Could you all please give Governor O'Malley one more round of applause for coming out today?" (More applause) "Thank you!" our president said, beaming as O'Malley continued to wave. "We will have the reception in the atrium now. All are welcome to attend."

Chairs moved as the crowd got up from their hot seats and made a beeline for the reception area. I waited a few minutes, letting the hoard of people around me stand up. I looked to my left. The attractive woman sitting there had already left. I cursed myself for not talking to her sooner. I stood up, stretching under the hot sun. I walked across the grass, up a small set of white steps, and into the fancy building, a cool breeze of air conditioning washing over me. The ceilings were high and the food looked expensive. Waiters buzzed around holding silver plates filled with foods that were hard to pronounce. I suddenly felt underdressed in my blue jeans and red t-shirt. I looked at the rest of the room, at the people dressed in button- ups and summer dresses, and wondered if I should leave. Then our president walked in—and another thought occurred. I stood for a second as I watched him get wrapped up by an eager middle-aged woman. He smiled and spoke animatedly as I waited for her to go away. Within moments I realized that the only way I was going to break up his conversation before all the food was gone was by personally interrupting. I looked around for better options, spotting one quickly. Adrienne Jones, Governor O'Malley's friend and Speaker Pro Tem of the Maryland House of

Delegates, was standing directly across from me, making her way to some of the food. I started to walk towards her then noticed our president. It looked like he was wrapping up his conversation, the woman he was talking with shook his hand and started to walk away. I looked at him, then back at Adrienne, before making my decision. "Hello," I said, walking up to my target. "How are you doing?"

"I'm doing well." Delegate Jones said cheerily.

"I really enjoyed your speech," I said. "I just wanted to thank you for paving the way for black men and women like myself," I said. "Working hard and getting good grades is difficult enough; having to deal with the added pressure of racism is no piece of cake."

"I'm just glad I was able to have an impact." Delegate Jones said, picking up a sliver of diced pineapple. "You'd be surprised," she said. "It was hard being black at that time, but it was just as hard being a woman. Men—black ones, too, did not like seeing me in college. But I am glad we have come to a place where equality is valued."

"I agree," I said, hatching my plan. "I know you and Governor O'Malley have been working on the Question 6 Campaign in Maryland which will legalize same sex marriage," I said. "Question 6 to me is the closest thing we have to the Civil Rights movement of the '60s. I know some of the hardships are different, but the human rights of it are similar."

"Yes, they are," said Delegate Jones. "What we're trying to get across is that all love is equal, and that we do not have the legal right to put a sanction on it."

"I understand," I said. "I was actually adopted by a lesbian couple who echoed that same message. They taught me to educate people who did not understand that sentiment. If possible, I would like to be a part of the campaign."

"I think that would be magnificent," Delegate Jones said. "To have someone who is a… an actual voice of and product of a same-sex household," she stuttered, "helps put a face on the issue. As a delegate, I can say a lot of great things, but I haven't *lived it* in the same way that you have. I am doing a radio interview the week before the election on Question 6. Would you be interested in being a part of that?" She asked.

"Yes, I would," I said sheepishly.

"Great," Delegate Jones said firmly. "Before that, there is a fundraiser that Governor O'Malley is throwing. I'll put your name on the list and will let him know who you are. At the event we can discuss what your role in the campaign will be."

"Thanks," I said.

"Thank *you*." Delegate Jones said. "Here is my card." She passed it to me and said, "Write your email and phone number on the back and I will contact you in the coming weeks about the fundraiser. The radio interview is on November 1st.

"I'll be there," I said confidently.

"Excellent," Delegate Jones said as a woman slid beside me, the same look in her eye that had been in mine minutes earlier. "It looks like this woman would like to speak to you as well so I'll let her get to it," I said as the woman smiled appreciatively. "It was nice meeting you," I said, shaking Delegate Jones hand lightly. "It was nice meeting you too, Tony," she said. "We'll be in touch."

I smiled in what I hoped was a warm, non-threatening way, before making a show of checking out a quiche I had no intention of eating as I walked out of the building.

I retreated up the grass hill and made it back into the parking lot, looking around like a deer in headlights for my silver car. Five seconds later I spotted it hiding behind a black SUV. I sauntered over to it and opened the door, sliding into my seat. I started the car, but did not

move. *I wish it was November now* I thought *(even though I hate the cold)*. I felt like a kid who

had just confirmed a date with the girl of his dreams 2 months in advance. It felt great, but it

needed to hurry up and happen. I turned on the AC and put the car in reverse, swooping around

and driving out the parking lot, eager to meet what lay in store.

Chapter 35: Fifteen Minutes

It was late October. Leaves were turning pretty colors and the temperature was dropping. A presidential election was up for grabs. The nation seemed more split than ever. The counterculture had gone mainstream.

In Maryland another battle raged; this one on same-sex marriage. On November 4th, residents would go to the polls to cast their vote on whether or not same-sex marriage would become law. One week before the election, the polls clocked the issue at a 50/50 spilt among voters. Arguments for both sides were in full swing. Same-sex marriage was either a human right or breaking with tradition. It was either proof of America's growth or a precursor to its downfall. I watched every ad with vigor, storing arguments to use for the radio interview. Both sides had good points, and I could see why the polls were close, even in the liberal state of Maryland.

I stayed in on Halloween night to get a good night's rest. When I woke up the next day the interview still seemed far away. I would not get a chance to speak until 4:00 p.m. I tried to go through my normal routine. I ate my early-morning yogurt, exercised, showered, then settled in front of the TV to watch *Sportscenter*. *So this is my day,* I said to myself. *This is my day until 4:00 p.m.* My phone buzzed. A message from my friend Valon appeared, wishing me good luck. I responded promptly then set the phone down, thinking.

Today represents a step in my evolution, I thought dramatically. *Today, I will be coming out.* I was right though. It was, and I would. I had told my friends that my parents were gay, scolded some of them for using the word "faggot" in everyday speech. But I had never made a case for gay rights in front of them. I was scared that was too far. Today I would leave that fear behind. It was time to stop hiding.

I drove off to the nearby CVS to kill some time. By the time I got back, it was only noon. I groaned then looked at my backpack, opening one of my Sociology books. I studied the same material over and over, forcing myself to focus on something else. Two hours later, it was finally time to start getting ready. I rushed upstairs, slipping on a pair of loafers and a button-down shirt. I brushed my woolly hair a few times then raced back downstairs, closing the door quickly behind me. Somehow I was running on time; which was not a good thing. I had planned to be at least 30 minutes early so I could mentally prepare while there. I thought about how tired I was as I hopped into my silver car, reversing down the gravel driveway and spinning onto the road. I fiddled with my phone, turning the GPS on while I drove. A robotic, feminine voice guided me as I tried my best not to get lost. Thirty minutes later I arrived—on time. I hopped out of the car and walked into the building, spotting a friendly receptionist by the front counter.

"Hi," I said. "My name is Anthony Hynes."

"Yes," the woman said. "We've been expecting you," she said eerily. "Adrienne actually called to tell us that she is running a little late due to traffic on 95 north, but should be here in the next 20 minutes or so."

"Okay," I said, sitting down in an old chair by the front desk. I started to take in the studio as time passed, looking at the high ceilings and vibrant walls.

This place is pretty cool, I thought. Suddenly the door swung open, revealing Delegate Jones, who looked stressed but energized. "Sorry I'm late," she said. "That traffic is ridiculous."

"It's fine and I know," I said.

"Okay," She said. "You ready?"

"Yup," I said.

"Excellent," she said, checking her watch. "Bryan should be coming out shortly."

Adrienne looked around, searching for Bryan. A few seconds later a slender, middle-aged black man strolled into the room.

"Hi, I'm Bryan," he said to me, shaking my hand firmly.

"Tony. It's nice to meet you," I said, shaking his hand firmly back.

"Okay, well you guys can follow me back to the studio," he said. We walked past futuristic looking cubicles on our way. I started to feel anxious. "Just around this corner—yup" Bryan said as Delegate Jones and I walked through a small door. "And here we are," Bryan said. I looked around at the room, four swivel chairs, four sets of headphones, and a switchboard sat around a lopsided white table. I stared at the headphones, realizing that in a few minutes, hundreds (or 20 or 30) people would hear my voice. There would be no retakes.

"Ok, so. *To*-ny. " He said, placing emphasis on the first syllable. "So—I just need to go over a few things before we start."

"No problem," I said, glancing at Delegate Jones.

"So," Bryan began. "Your given name is Anthony Hynes? Correct?"

"Yes," I answered.

"And would you rather be called by Tony or Anthony?" He said.

"Tony is fine," I said.

"Great," he said. "All right, and you were adopted by two women?"

"Yes," I said.

"And those two women were white?" He said inquisitively.

"Yes." I said, beginning to wonder how much of my bio he had actually read.

"Okay," he said. "And at what age did you start living with your two moms?"

"I was three," I said calmly.

"Excellent. My apologies," he said, motioning to the rest of the room. "This is Ryan, and this is Tisha," he said, pointing to a round middle-aged man and an attractive 30-something-year-old black woman on the other side of the room. "They will be joining us for this discussion as well."

"Hi," Tisha and Ryan said in unison, waving to me.

"I think your story is really interesting," Tisha said.

"Thanks," I said, briefly glancing at Ryan, who sat there, stone faced.

"So here's how the show works," Bryan said. "I am going to introduce you, and then you're going to say a few words about yourself. Try to make your initial statement brief."

"Okay" I said.

"By the way," he said. "Hold the headphones to your ears like this," he said, pressing the headphones hard to his ears. "And speak directly into the mic. Yeah, like that," he said as I mimicked speaking into the device.

"So after you introduce yourself," he said, "Delegate Jones will speak about the Question 6 campaign in Maryland?"

"Yes." Delegate Jones chimed in.

"Okay—and after she speaks, we will take a few questions from our listeners."

"Great," I said as Bryan strapped on his headset like a soldier ready for battle. I picked up my headphones, strapping them to my ears as the room around me muted itself.

"*Five, four, three, two, one*, someone on the outside of our paned glass mimed to Bryan as he shifted in his chair. "Good afternoon!" Bryan said, waving off the man outside of the glass. "It is November first, 2012, just a few days before Election Day, so make sure to go out and vote!" He declared.

"Today we will be talking about Question 6, one of the hottest-debated topics on the ballot this year," he said. "For those of you who haven't been paying attention, Question 6 is an item on the ballot this year that if passed, will legalize gay marriage in the State of Maryland. Some of us believe that if the bill is passed it would be a step back for our country while others believe that it should be passed because gay marriage is a human right. The Gay Rights Movement in this country has been compared to the Civil Rights Movement of the 1960s, carried out by our black leaders. However, many believe that the two are not comparable. That the fight for freedom endured by the men and women shot and stabbed while standing in voting lines is different than the hardships faced by the gay population today. Today to speak on the matter we have Adrienne Jones, Current Speaker Pro Tem of the Maryland House of Delegates, and Tony Hynes, a college student at UMBC adopted by two white women. Tony is also black," Bryan added. "He will introduce himself, and talk about some of his experiences growing up in that lifestyle. Afterwards, we will take some calls from you and have a discussion about the issue in question. But without further ado, here is Tony to start things off." Bryan motioned to me, holding up three fingers, then two, then one. I took the hint.

"Good afternoon," I said, attempting to make my voice deeper than it was. "First I would like to thank Bryan and 103.7 for being such gracious hosts and inviting us to speak today," I said, pausing.

"I was adopted at the age of five by two women who happened to be lesbians. Without them I would not be the strong, intelligent man I am today," I said. "At the time they adopted me, gay marriage was not legal in any state. We were a family, but were not recognized under the law as such. We were not entitled to some of the same federal benefit programs as traditional heterosexual-headed households. When one of my moms died of cancer, my mother Janet was unable to collect Social Security for me because they were not a married couple.

"It's more than just tradition versus non tradition," I said. "It's about recognizing families under the law so they can receive the same benefits others are granted. However..." I said as Bryan gave me a signal to hurry up, "One thing I hear all the time is that being raised by gay people messes kids up—that it has the potential to make them gay. I could talk about how social science research has proven that theory to be universally false. I could talk about my thesis research on the subject that shows that children from gay-headed households have been found to be more well-adjusted, and more open to diversity than their peers from heterosexual-headed households.

"However, that is not what I am here for. I am here to talk about my own experiences." I paused, looking for words to fill the space. "I am the first person in my biological family to go to college. I have friends that are Black, Asian, Native-American, White, and Latino. They come from two-parent households, single-parent households, religious households, and non-religious households. They all accept me. They all accept my moms. We have mutual respect for one another, and for one another's families.

"When I told them my moms were gay, most of them didn't even care, and that is honestly the reaction I get from a lot of people. Yes, my upbringing was different than other kids. Yes, people do ask me questions about my moms. But it is almost to gain... more knowledge about a family structure they haven't seen before than to ostracize or condemn my family," I said as Bryan shifted in his seat.

"Thank you, Tony," he chimed in, clearly perturbed I was over my time limit. "That was very insightful. And now, Delegate Jones, would you like to say a few words?" Bryan asked hazily.

"Yes," Delegate Jones began. "Adding on to what Tony said, I would like to point out that passing Question 6 is about stopping discrimination. We need to make sure that all Marylanders know that we stand with them. Right now, an entire population is considered an *other*. They do not have the same workplace benefits, housing benefits, life insurance benefits, and Social Security benefits as their peers. Question 6 is about making sure that we level the playing field, and that we hear their voice," she said.

"I along with Governor O'Malley am committed to making sure that people understand that Question 6 is not about forcing an agenda on people. It is about honoring families like Tony's."

"Thank you, Delegate Jones," Bryan said. "Some of us do feel like there is an agenda being forced upon us. That something that is not normal is being considered normal to further political campaigns. However, we will take a short break, and come back and get some feedback from you guys at home." Bryan took off his headphones as hip-hop played throughout the room.

"That was good," Delegate Jones said, turning to me.

"Thanks," I said. "I liked what you said, too." The music faded out as Bryan clapped his headphones back on, scooting forward in his chair, puffing his chest out.

"Good afternoon," he said. "We are back—and here to discuss Question 6. Today, we have with us Delegate Adrienne Jones and Tony Hynes, a child of same-sex adoption. Right now, we would like to hear from you at home about this issue.

"Do you think same-sex marriage should be legal in Maryland?" Bryan asked. "Do you think the preachers and pastors supporting this same-sex marriage item are betraying their values? Is same sex marriage a slippery slope?" he finished.

"Hello!" Bryan said, pushing a red button.

"Yeah, my name is Fred," a faraway voice said. "I just think this same-sex marriage is another example of America getting further and further away from its Christian roots. And Question 6 is just another example of them trying to change marriage. Marriage is between a man and a woman, not a man and a man."

"Thank you, Fred," Bryan said as a phone disconnected. "You're on." Bryan said energetically as another caller's voice rang in my ears.

"Hello, yes, this is Tom," he said. "I completely agree with the last caller. These so-called ministers and these so-called black leaders should be ashamed of themselves for promoting this agenda. They act as though this isn't a sin, as though it is not an abomination. The Bible specifically states that marriage is between a man and a woman. That's just how it is," he said. "A man and a man cannot claim to be a married couple because they are not a married couple. God made a man and a woman for each other. If gays wanna live their lifestyle on their own time that's their business—but to say under law that what they do is not only *okay*, but that they can have the same rights granted to married couples, *real* married couples, is just plain wrong. This country is fading fast."

"Thank you, Tom!" Bryan interjected. "You made a good point. Many of our black leaders, our pastors, even our mayor, have supported Question 6, a law that contradicts what they once stood for. They are acting like puppets for the mainstream media, and they think that no one will call them out. I am glad that there are those like Ted willing to call them on them on their dishonesty, on their contradiction."

I looked directly at Bryan, itching for a chance to respond. "And next we have Larry!" He uttered as I shot him what I hoped was a polite but pointed glance.

"Hello," Larry said as Bryan looked away from me. "That young man on there— umm..."

"*Tony,*" Bryan interjected.

"Yeah, Tony." Larry said. "So, *Tony*—you were raised by two women?"

"Yes," I said into the mic as if I were on trial.

"All right," Larry said slowly. "So it's like this, marriage is between a man and a woman. And it's between a man and a woman so that they can raise a child together. The boy needs a father and the girl needs a mother," he said. "That's the just the way it is. It's like a lion in the jungle. A little lion cub can't become a man without the lion guiding him. You wouldn't have two female lions in the jungle raising a child because the little lion cub would not know how to fend for himself or know what to do when danger arose. You see what I'm saying?" Larry asked.

"Yeeaaass," I said, not able to keep the annoyance out of my voice.

"Right," he said, "so your moms could have been the greatest people in the world. But that does not make it right. Lion cubs need a mother and a father."

"Thank you, Larry!" Bryan boomed. "We're going to take a short break but we will be taking callers afterwards, so keep those phone lines open." He put down his headphones as a Beyoncé song blared from the speakers.

"Hey," I said. "I would like to respond to that last caller."

238

"Okay," Bryan said. "Let's get another caller in and then you can respond to that last one after."

"Okay," I said firmly, sitting back stiffly in my chair.

"Thank you to all of our callers for holding!" Bryan yelled as the song ended. "Next up we have…"

"Roger," a man interjected.

"Yes, and Roger?" Bryan asked. "Have you been listening to our discussion?" "Yes, I have," Roger said. "I just think gays are a blight on our community. If it were up to me, they would all be sent to an island somewhere. This gay marriage thing is a joke. So if me and a frog get legally licensed to marry, that counts, too?" He said rhetorically.

"Okay," Bryan said, laughing loudly. "Thank you, Roger. Yes, next caller," he said, avoiding my gaze.

"Yes, my name is April," the caller said. "I just wanted to say that you people calling in, all you men—ought to be ashamed of yourselves. You talk about how gays are sinning and this and that but you all probably sit at home all day watching porn and gambling. This man, Tony Hynes, has obviously done something positive with his life. Whether or not I agree or disagree with gay marriage, it is obvious that his moms did a good job raising him. In Jesus' name we are all sinners, and we do not have the right to judge people, only God can do that," she said.

"People like you—all the men who called in, are an embarrassment to other Christians. You are the people who make other Christians look bad, who make us look like we are bigots. If two people love each other, I say let them be. Who are they hurting?" She declared more than asked. "They're not hurting me. I know that. They're not hurting the men who called in, either," she said. "Thank you," she said, hanging up the phone.

"April, we just feel as though marriage is between a man a woman, and that it should stay that way," Bryan interjected, forgetting to thank April for calling. "To our listeners at home—get out and vote. Do the right thing." Bryan motioned to me. "I think Tony would like to say a few words as well."

"Yes," I said, trying to figure out how to respond to every caller in one breath. "First I would like to say that God is love. Gay marriage is about love. Nothing else. It's about two people who care for each other coming together. Do the right thing. Vote for love."

My words sounded corny, like a campaign slogan, and so I added more. "And to those who think that gay marriage will change America. To those who think that gays can't raise kids. It already has, and we're already here. There is a whole generation of kids just like me. The change you fear has already taken place, and we are not a weaker nation for it. We have heard from the parents within same-sex headed households. We have heard from the opponents of same-sex marriage. Who we have not heard from as much are the kids of same sex couples," I said.

"But we are starting to, and in the coming years I can guarantee that we will hear more. My friends from same-sex headed households will tell you the some of the same things I said today: that they were raised to respect others, and to be the best people they could be. We, the children of same-sex couples, didn't grow up in some crazy 'lifestyle'; we come from normal families. And we want our families to be recognized, we want to have the same rights your family has," I said.

"Thank you, Tony," Bryan added solemnly. "Well, that about wraps up our show."

"Annnd," Delegated Jones interrupted, "Please remember to go out and vote for Question 6 this Tuesday. We have a chance to be on the right side of history. We are up in the polls, but it's a close race," she said. "Pastors, politicians, regular citizens, and first-time voters have all stood up and supported Question 6 because it is about telling our children that they will not be discriminated against based upon who they love. Stand with us."

"Thank you, Delegate Jones," Bryan said. "Remember to go out and vote! They call Question 6 'marriage equality', but in reality it is a referendum on marriage and on the tradition of marriage," he said. "Keep that in mind when you go out and vote Tuesday. The Bible defines marriage as between a man a woman, and God frowns upon same-sex relationships. Remember that before you go to the polls."

"Also remember that God is love," I said. "And that this is what same-sex marriage and Question 6 is about. It is about allowing two people to love each other fully. Go out and vote *for* Question 6," I reiterated for emphasis.

"Thanks, Tony!" Bryan said.

"Well, that concludes our show today!" Bryan shouted. "I would like to thank Tony and Delegate Jones again for being on our program."

"Thank you for having us," Delegate Jones said.

"Yes, Thank you," I added.

"It was our pleasure," Bryan said. "To our listeners at home, don't forget to vote on Question 6, but also remember to study up on the candidates you would like to vote for. Do your research. We are going to take a quick commercial break and then we will be back with an hour of commercial-free music for you," he said. "Stay tuned." He took his headphones off, drawing his chair back, before standing up. "Thanks again, guys, that was great," he said like a boxing promoter after a prizefight.

"No problem," I said, "Thank you again for having us."

"No problem," he said. "We might do another segment on this before the election. Would you like to come back for that?"

"Sure," I said.

"Great," Bryan said. "I'll email you more of the details later."

"Delegate Jones," he said, addressing Adrienne. "It was very nice having you on the show as well." He smiled at her then shook her hand softly.

"Thank you for having us," Delegate Jones said. "This is an important discussion."

"Yes, it is," Bryan said, smiling. "Hopefully next time we will have more time to talk." He was addressing the discussion, but from his tone, it sounded as though he was hinting at something else. I looked at Delegate Jones as she smiled politely.

"Have a nice day," she said.

"You, too," Bryan said, showing all of his sparkling white teeth. The delegate picked up her purse as I stood up.

"Bye, thanks for coming," the 30-something-year-old woman said as I walked out. "No problem," I said, smiling curtly. I looked at Ryan, who nodded solemnly as I followed Delegate Jones out of the door and back down the hall. She remained silent as we walked past the receptionist and out of the door. I raced ahead of her to hold the door as she weaved her way through the doorway, and before I knew it we were back in the crisp fall air.

"That was ridiculous," she said as we stepped over the small rocks of a gravel parking lot. "Yeah," I said. "Kinda felt like an ambush at times."

"That is not how a host is supposed to act," Delegate Jones said. "A host is supposed to be the mediator—the moderator, of the discussion. He is not supposed to give his opinion. Bryan was all over the place. He said he wanted to have a discussion but he was the only one talking at times. He seemed more concerned with pushing his own agenda, his own thoughts, than letting the other side make their case. I'm sorry," she said. "I knew the radio station was a little more conservative, but I had no idea Bryan would be like that."

"It's okay," I said. "I've met people like him before. Some of the people who called in had some—interesting perspectives as well," I said with a smirk.

"Them too!" Delegate Jones said. "It's one thing to hold an opinion, but it's a whole other thing to disrespect an entire group like that. Some of those men sounded bigoted, and that woman was right to call them out the way she did. They sit around drinking and doing other stuff all day and try to judge someone else.

"Like the pastors say, God is the only judge, and the only person who has the right to condemn a person," she said. "They just don't like homosexuality, thinks it's gross, and wanted to find a reason to justify their bigotry," she said coldly. "Thank you for coming on the show with me today though," she added, "you were great."

"Thanks," I said. "Honestly, what those men were saying is not different than some of the stuff I have heard my whole life. I mean—the difference today is that all of that talk was concentrated into one *45-minute segment.* It was okay though, I had fun."

It was true, I was not thrilled at what some of the callers had said, but I was thankful that there were still people out there who would publicly admonish my upbringing. Everyone was so PC, so tempered, so...*boring.* It was nice to debate again, to be able to defend my moms' honor. Secretly, I had hoped that the callers would be a little nasty. I was sick of people saying that America was turning gay. I was sick of people saying that no one cared. I was sick of people downplaying my story and stories like it.

I lied on the air when I said our family was normal. It was not normal. It was unique. The people in it were normal. But some of the world did not see us that way. I was glad some of that world was highlighted, and I was quite pleased that they had made fools of themselves on a far-reaching radio station. I was glad my friends had a chance to witness it as well. The fact that friends—both okay and undecided on the concept of homosexuality—all stated how backwards some of the callers were invigorated me. But more than anything, it made me feel as though I was part of a completely new generation. A generation that was ready for families like mine to be normal.

Chapter 36: The New Normal

The moment I knew how much I had changed when it came to my moms did not take place at the radio station. That event only solidified it. No; the actual event actually happened weeks earlier, at the fundraiser I was invited to by Delegate Jones.

It was a crisp October night and I was unsure of what to wear. I had a nice lavender dress shirt, but I did not know if that was enough. *The Governor will be there,* I told myself, *maybe I should just play it safe with a suit.* I grabbed a blue striped tie, plucked a floral dress shirt from the dresser, and located my wrinkled slacks by the back of my closet. *This'll do,* I thought, putting each item on. I examined myself in the mirror, upset at my failure to shave. *Whatever,* I thought, *this'll have to do.* I put my charcoal grey suit jacket on, turned off the light, and left the room in a huff, plugging the address into my phone. I looked at the phone's directions briefly as I always did, ignoring which exit I should take in favor of looking at the time I was scheduled to arrive. *Right on time.* I told myself, looking the GPS arrival time. *Maybe even a little bit early.* I closed the front door of the house, locked up, and hopped into my small car, reversing on the rain-soaked gravel.

Thirty-five minutes later I was there, shuffling through some dive bar in downtown Baltimore. I looked to my left and right. Everyone had jeans and a T-shirt on. I started to panic. "Excuse me," I said to a red-faced bartender. "I'm looking for the fundraiser?"

"Yeah," she said, looking me up and down, "It's upstairs, just go around that corner there and you'll see a couple steps."

"Thanks," I said, walking towards a big red sign in the back.

"Just around there," she said as I paused in front of it. I peered around the sign and spotted the winding staircase hidden from view.

"Thanks," I said again, heading towards the steps. I made haste of walking up the stairs, still worried that I was not in the right place. I reached the top step and immediately realized how wrong that assumption was.

I had stumbled onto a plush, hidden floor. With its high ceilings, shiny floors, and mahogany chairs, the room resembled the White House Correspondents Dinner more than it did the bar downstairs. The people, with their tailored suits and white teeth, matched the room. Bright lights flashed throughout as men with microphones crowded around a burly man with too much make up on his face.

"This is an important issue for me—"he said. "You know, it's important to let people know that it's not okay to discriminate against others because of whom they are or who they love." Camera bulbs whooshed and snapped as he spoke, each photographer eager to capture every facial expression.

"Growing up, I was exposed to a lot of diversity," he said. "When my father was in college he was an RA on a floor with several lesbian and gay couples. When I was there I got to experience those varying relationship sets and I just began to see it as normal. I began to see that these were hardworking, kind individuals, who were always nice to me and gracious towards my father. Realizing that diversity is important, and realizing that you have to treat others the way you want to be treated—is what Question 6 is all about. I am glad that we have a governor who realizes that, and is willing to fight to make sure that happens."

The camera panned to Governor O'Malley, who waved from somewhere beside the cheese dip.

"Thank you, Brendon," two men said in unison as they holstered their cameras.

"You're welcome," he said politely, his towering frame hovering over them.

I sidestepped him and fluttered to the back of the room, trying my best to blend in. I was a little off, a little nervous. I could feel it. A couple of people started looking at me from around the stairs. They made their way toward me, two big smiles on their faces. Their mouths started moving.

"What's up, man!" they said when they were 3 feet away, closing in.

"Not much," I said happily, glad to shake hands with my friends. "Yeah, man, sorry for the lateness; got completely lost for a little while," Troy said, his shoulder-length Native-American hair gathered neatly in a ponytail.

"No problem, man," I said, "thanks for coming."

"Wouldn't have missed it, man," he said, looking around the room. "Dude, this place is high class," he said, smirking.

"Yeah, man," Demetrius chimed in, adjusting his personality glasses. "What's up with my man Brendon Ayanbadejo, though?" He said, looking at the burly man. "He looks so much softer in person."

"Looks like a pretty boy with all that make-up on his face."

"Ha ha; yeah, man, he's definitely wearing lipstick," Troy said.

"Right!?" Demetrius said. "He's not making the Ravens proud right now with that look. Anyway, glad to be here though, man," he said. "Can you walk with me to the bar? Ya know— not 21 yet and don't know how they do things here," he said, laughing.

"Yeah, sucks for you, man," I said.

"Whatever, it's all good, though," he said, "in a couple months I'll be 21 and you won't be able to say shit."

"Yeah," I said, pausing. "I'll still find something," I said with a chuckle.

"Okay, whatever," Demetreius said, "Where is this bar?"

"It's over there, I think," I said, walking in the general direction.

"Cool," Demetrius said, following behind. Troy brought up the rear, clearly amused by everything happening around him. We stopped and stepped up to the counter like three men who knew they were a little out of their element.

"Could I have a...whiskey sour," I said, putting more bass in my voice than was necessary.

"Sure," the 40-something-year-old bartender said, glancing to my friends. "Would any of you like anything?"

"No thank you," Troy said. "No I'm good, thank you," Demetrius said. The bartender shot all of us a look and then trudged away to make the drink, vigorously smashing the ice cubes into the clear glass.

"Here you are," she said after a minute, thrusting the cup in my face. "That will be $14." I took my wallet out from my slacks and clumsily placed the money in her hands, paying an extra $4 for a tip she did not deserve. She ran back to the counter to ring it up as I slipped it to Demetrius.

"Thanks, man," he said.

"No problem, man," I said, glancing over at Governor O'Malley as he chatted up a couple of people in the middle of the bar. *Welp, might as well,* I told myself.

I tried to make my approach as unassuming as possible, sliding into his view as he finished a sentence. "Did you say Gonzaga?" I said casually.

"Yeah," Governor O'Malley said.

"Nice," I said, "my best friend went there."

"Oh, wow," he said, "what's his name?"

"Devin O'Reilly," I said.

"Hmm..." O'Malley said. "What his father's name?"

"Dennis," I said.

"Oh, yeah!" O'Malley said. "I didn't know Dennis but I remember the O'Reilly clan." *The O'Reilly's actually all went to St. Johns,* I thought to myself. *Meaning that I was mistaken—or that O'Malley was probably lying.* "I don't see many Irish-Catholic folk around these days," he said with a chuckle. "There's only one of us. It's always nice to hear about the Montgomery County area, though. I have good memories of that place."

"Yeah, I'm from Takoma Park," I said, "by Sligo."

"Yes," he said, "nice area."

"It is. But anyway, I actually just wanted to thank you for going to bat on the Question 6 issue," I said, getting to the point. "I was raised by two women, and understand some of the friction you have probably faced trying to get this passed. I have been working with Delegate Adrienne Jones on the campaign," I said, playing my hand up more than I needed to. "We have discussed ways I can help the campaign."

"Oh, umm—yes," Governor O'Malley said, "Adrienne is great, District...13?" He said, finding himself.

"Yes," I said.

"That is excellent," he said, nodding. "Are your moms here tonight?"

"No they are not," I said. "It's actually me and my mom now. One of them passed away."

"Well, I am very sorry to hear that," O'Malley said, looking deeply into my eyes.

"Thank you," I said. "How is everything going, though—in general I mean, how do you like being in office?"

He relaxed, his shoulders slumping. "I mean—it is what it is—ya know?" He asked as if I knew first-hand what the daily grind of being a governor was like.

"Yeah," I said off handedly. "Well—hang in there," I said awkwardly.

"Thanks," O'Malley said. "I'll try."

"Hey, Governor," a jubilant voice behind me said. *It's time to leave,* I thought. "Good luck," I said, shaking O'Malley's hand.

"Thanks," he said gruffly, looking me firmly in the eye. I walked past a new foosball table, around a small divot in the wood, and up to a set of chairs, where I spotted my next target.

"Hello," I said jovially. "My name is Tony Hynes. Delegate Jones told me to talk to you—you're Rick right?"

"Yes!" Rick said. "Come and have a seat." I looked for Troy and Demetrius, who looked to be in polite conversation by the bar. Rick followed my eyes. "Are those your friends?" He asked inquisitively.

"Yes," I said.

"Well, it's great that they came—I'm glad you brought them. Delegate Jones has told me all about you," he said. "I think you have an amazing story. You were really on the frontlines of this issue and have a unique perspective on things. First, I'd just like to ask you a couple of basic questions—is that okay?"

"Sure," I said, happy to have his attention.

"Yes," he said, his bald head gleaming under the high-powered lights. "Yes," he reiterated. "So at what age were you adopted?"

"I went to live with Mary and Janet when I was three," I said. "But I was not officially adopted until I was nineteen."

"Wow," Rick said. "And why was that?"

"Well," I said. "There was a long custody battle that made it difficult for either Mary or Janet to adopt me, so both of them became my legal guardians."

"Interesting," he said. "And you were the only child they took in?"

"Yes," I said.

"Thank you," he said. "Now, throughout the run-up to the election we may ask you to speak at an event or two—would you be comfortable with that?"

"Yes," I said firmly.

"Great, now—before that happens we need to prep a little bit. Like—let's go over some of what an opponent might say. I'll say it and then you answer," he said.

"Okay," I said.

"So here's an example," Rick said. *"Homosexuality is a sin, God forbids it, so why would we allow a law that goes against that?"* Rick paused, staring at me.

"Well," I began, "my moms always taught me that it's important to treat others the way you would like to be treated. In this case, that means that all people regardless of who they love should be entitled to the same rights. It's always important to remember that whatever your religion, God asks us to love one another the same, and that He is the only judge. It is up to us to treat each other with respect, to give one another the same rights, and let Him decide the rest."

"That was good," Rick said. "But we want to keep the focus more on rights and less on religion. If someone asks you a question on religion, you can say 'Question 6 is about retaining human rights for all people, regardless of their background.' You can leave it at that," he said. "We are not trying to change the minds of devoutly religious people." They are already set in their ways. Speaking to them for a couple hours is not going to change their viewpoint. No—who we're trying to reach are those undecided voters. Those who may have a gay neighbor or friend but aren't quite sure what their stance on the issue is," he said. "What we're trying to get them to do is to understand that their neighbors, their friends, just want the same rights as everybody else, and that it's that simple."

"I understand." I said.

"Great," he said. "So why don't we try that again?" I nodded. "*So,*" he said, making his voice deeper in what I assumed was his impersonation of a working-class person. "*I have a gay neighbor and a gay friend, and they seem just fine the way they are. I am not homophobic or bigoted, I just don't understand why they would need a piece of paper to tell them that they are married. I mean—if they love each other, they should not need that piece of paper to affirm their status—right?*" Rick stopped, looking at me.

"Well, I understand your viewpoint," I said, playing into the role. "I once felt the same way about my two moms. I did not understand why they needed a court-assigned paper to tell them that they were married."

"However," I said. "As I grew older I realized that there were other reasons for having that piece of paper. No—my moms didn't need that paper. Yes—they loved each other. But, without that piece of paper there were many things that they were not entitled to, which they *would* have had, had they been considered a married couple by law. When my mother died, for instance, my mom was not able to collect Social Security benefits for me because they were not a married couple. When I needed to go to the doctor, Janet had to get a signed note from Mary, because Mary was the only one who was able to be granted parental rights, because Janet and Mary did not have joint custody rights as heterosexual adoptive parents had. Simple things like that really affect a family during some of their darkest hours," I said. "That's why passing Question 6 is so important. It gives families like mine equal protection under the law, in addition to acknowledging the love that exists within our households."

"That was good," Rick said. "We can definitely build on that. Telling the audience about your upbringing while answering those types of questions really helps us. It's important for the public to be able to put a face with this vote, and families like yours are great for that."

"Glad to help in any way possible," I said.

"Excellent," he said. "We're actually shooting a commercial tonight—just a 30- second spot highlighting some same-sex families. If you're interested we can head over to Cindy to get things started."

"Let's do it," I said cheerfully.

"Great," Rick said, folding his notebook, "she's right over here." He stood up, his loafers clacking on the wood floor as I followed behind. "Cindy, this is Tony," he said, marching up to a fit blond woman in her thirties. "He grew up with two moms."

"Oh wow—great to meet you," Cindy said, shaking my hand firmly.

"Nice to meet you," I said, smiling.

"Oh"—she said, "how rude of me. This is my husband Jake," nodding for him to walk over. We exchanged greetings, firmly shook hands, the corners of my mouth beginning to twitch from all the smiling it was doing.

"Yes," Cindy said, interrupting our interaction. "So this commercial, as Rick may have told you, "is going to be all about Question 6. We want to show people the love that exists within these families and get them fired up to vote on Tuesday. Whenever you're ready," she said. "We can get started. Do you need anything or have any questions? ".

"Umm—yes," I said, glancing back at the bar. "Can my friends be in it?"

"Sure!" She said brightly.

"Great," I said, "let me go over and get them," I said. She smiled politely as I walked away, retreating back to the area around the bar.

"'Sup man," Demetrius said.

"Not much," I said.

"Clearly that's a lie," Troy interjected. "My man is out here being a boss."

"Ha ha, whatever man," I said. "*We're* out here."

"Yeah, yeah, whatever man," Troy said, smirking, "we all are but tonight you're doing your thing."

"Yeah," Demetrius said. "Who was that guy you were talking to?"

"He's affiliated with the campaign," I said. "He was talking to me about other ways I can get involved."

"Nice," Demetrius said.

"Yeah"—I said. "He actually wants me to be a part of this commercial they're doing for the campaign. You guys wanna join me?"

"In what—the commercial?" Demetrius said.

"Yeah man." I said.

"Umm—naw; I'm good," Demetrius said.

"Yeah I'll think I'll pass too, man," Troy said. "We're your friends and all, but tonight is about you and the perspective you bring. All the attention should be on you. Plus, if I appear with you we're *going* to look like a gay couple, man. Which is *cool* and all—nothing wrong with that… but that's not us and would take away from your message. Like—there is no other way to put that," he added with a chuckle. "So go do your thing, man."

"You sure?" I said.

"Yeah man," Troy said. I looked at Demetrius.

"I was gonna say what Troy said," he said. "This is your night and I don't wanna intrude. Do your thing."

"Okay," I said, "more for me." The two of them smiled as I began to walk away, a smile on my face.

"They're going to pass." I said, walking up to the blond woman. She frowned in what looked to be mock disappointment.

"They sure?" she asked.

"Yeah." I said. "They're camera shy."

"Oooooh," she said, pouting. "Well, let me get you ready," she said, grabbing a napkin from her bra. "You're a little shiny… there… much better," she said, dabbing my forehead. "Now I need you to stand right…*here,"* she said, lightly pushing me toward a spot marked with an X on the floor. "Perfect. Now I need you to look directly at that flashing red light." I strained my eyes, squinting at the annoying light. "Great," she said as her husband steadied the camera. "Now, we've been having people do these little snippets. The tagline has been 'I'm *for* Question 6.' You can play around with that any way you'd like," she said, smiling suggestively. *This woman is flirtatious,* I thought to myself. "You ready?" she said.

"Yes," I said, lying.

"Okay," she said, "we're rolling in three—two—one, *go,"* she said as the camera zoomed in on my face.

"I'm *for* Question 6," I said, suddenly very conscious of how dry my mouth was.

"Okay," she said. "That was okay, but we need you to—"here," she said, putting one hand on my stomach and the other on my back. "You're slouching just a little bit, draw your chest out—yup, that's it," she said as I complied.

"Perfect," she said. "I like your tone, but we need a little more emphasis on *for.* Also remember to smile!" She said enthusiastically. "Okay, we're on again in three—two—*one."* She said as a bright yellow light shined down on me.

"I'm *for* Question 6," I said as the light intensified, smiling as broadly as I could. "Great!" she said, "but I need your eyes over here," she said, gesturing toward the flashing red light. "Excellent," she said, as I adjusted my gaze. "Okay," she said, "we're on again in three—two—one, *go."*

"I'm *for* Question 6," I said enthusiastically into the camera, wearing the brightest smile I could muster. "That was great!" She said. I nodded, a pang of disappointment washing over me. *None of these words are my own, I thought to myself, I feel like a puppet. Why did I smile so big?*

I looked at Troy and Demetrius, both of them looking at me as though they did not recognize the person standing before them.

"Excuse me," I said. "I'd like to change things up a bit—can we do another take?"

"Sure," she said, motioning to her husband to get the camera ready.

"We're on again in three, two, one…"

I inhaled shallowly, preparing my lungs.

"I'm *for* my two moms." I said as the camera rolled on, smiling genuinely. "That was excellent," she said. "Why don't we roll that one more time…"

"Okay," I said.

On again in three, two, one…

"I'm **for** my two moms," I said more forcefully than before, a smile attached to my cheeks.

"Great! How'd you like that?"

"That was good." I said.

"Here," she said, motioning me over. "Come and have a look." I stepped off of the X and towards the red flashing light as it faded from view, huddling up next to her. A clicking noise was heard as she pressed a button on the camera. "…**for** my two moms," a deep voice repeated back to me. "Nice?" She said inquisitively.

"Looks good," I said.

"Great," she said, "we'll go with that. Thanks so much!" She said, hugging me. "What's your email?" she said. "I'll message you when it's done—should be a couple of weeks." I slid out a pen and found a napkin, writing my address down. "Thanks!" she said as I passed it to her. "Thanks to you guys as well!" She exclaimed, walking a few paces to hug Troy and Demetrius. "You guys are good friends!" she said. "Enjoy the rest of your night."

"Thanks," all of us said a few seconds apart, nodding as she walked off.

"That woman was—"

"I know," I said interrupting Demetrius. He chuckled, "That was really good though man," he said, switching subjects. "I was a *little* worried at first."

"Yeah, me too," Troy said, "it felt like they were trying to use you or something. But that last slogan was really good. Did you come up with up with that?"

"Yeah," I said, "it just kinda popped into my head."

"Nice, man," Troy said. "I'm proud of you. Always knew you were a politician!" he laughed.

"Yeah, right?" Demetrius said, smirking.

"Hynes 2046," I said sarcastically, chuckling.

We left an hour later, our bellies full and our minds no longer sober. *This was definitely one of the better nights of my life,* I thought to myself as we departed. *It wasn't just that I was able to get my message across—it was that my friends were there with me.* Forever it had felt like I had to fight the fight alone. Now I knew I did not. I had friends who were willing to be there when I needed them—friends who weren't adverse to change.

I had always known that there were those on my side, those willing to fight the good fight. But I had always cherished the minds of the neutral voters more, those who had probably not considered what it meant to be gay in America very often. My friends were some of those neutrals. To see them there was like having Christmas come early. They had always supported me, but this time they were actively putting themselves in the room with same-sex couples.

They were holding polite conversation with those in the room. They were trying. They were succeeding. I was proud of *them,* and I was proud of my message. It was simple. I was *for* my two moms, and I always would be.

Epilogue

That Tuesday, Maryland passed Question 6 and the Defense of Marriage Act was declared unconstitutional. Same-sex couples in the state were allowed to be married by law, subject to the same rights and benefits as their heterosexual married counterparts. Celebrations went on throughout the state, marriage equality stickers proudly affixed to car bumpers. I was thrilled, but another portrait still lingered in my mind. A few days prior, I had talked to my neighbor Kevin, his baritone voice still ringing in my ears.

I remember when you were **this** *high,* he had said, laying his palm flat on an invisible chair. *I remember that cute social worker you had too. She was so cute, I remember wanting to take her into the house and..." trailing off. "But anyway, so I remember the day Mary and Janet won the appeal that said you could stay with them. I remember your social worker that day. She was outside your house just bawling her eyes out. I went over to ask her what was wrong and she just kept crying. She told me,* **I don't know if they can raise him. He won't know how to be a man, or that he's black.**

"So I'm hugging her," Kevin says. "And I just keep telling her 'Don't worry, Tony's gonna be just fine. You watch, he's gonna be just fine. He's got two great people to make sure of that and he's got me, too. He's gonna be just fine.'"

Kevin's words echoed in my head. I smiled—*Just fine, indeed.*